HOCUS JOKUS

How to Do Funny Magic
by Steve Charney

Meadowbrook Press
Distributed by Simon & Schuster
New York

Library of Congress Cataloging-in-Publication Data
Charney, Steve.
   Hocus jokus : How to do funny magic / by Steve Charney.
      p. cm.
Summary: Describes the various aspects of performing as a magician and includes jokes and instructions for fifty funny magic tricks.
Includes bibliographical references (p.) and index.
   ISBN 0-88166-376-X (Meadowbrook) ISBN 0-684-01866-7 (Simon & Schuster)
  1. Magic tricks—Juvenile literature. 2. Wit and humor, Juvenile. [1. Magic tricks. 2. Jokes.
3. Wit and humor.] I. Title: How to do funny magic. II. Title.
   GV1548 .C43 2003
   793.8—dc21
                        2002009689

Editorial Director: Christine Zuchora-Walske
Proofreader: Megan McGinnis, Angela Wiechmann
Art Director: Peggy Bates
Desktop Publishing: Lisa Beller
Production Manager: Paul Woods
Cover Art and Illustrations: Blanche Sims
Index: Beverlee Day

Published by Meadowbrook Press, 5451 Smetana Drive, Minnetonka, Minnesota 55343

www.meadowbrookpress.com

BOOK TRADE DISTRIBUTION by Simon and Schuster, a division of Simon and Schuster, Inc., 1230 Avenue of the Americas, New York, New York 10020

08 07 06 05 04 03   10 9 8 7 6 5 4 3 2

Printed in the United States of America

Dedication

To Hank Neimark, who knows the true meaning of being a goofball

Acknowledgments

I'm going to keep this short, because no one reads acknowledgments anyway—except people who want to see if they're being thanked or who think they know people who are being thanked. And of course, some folks might skim this page quickly for famous names or funny names, such as Marvin T. Finklebone—who, by the way, is not being thanked here. I'm just using him as an example of someone who might be thanked if he existed—which I doubt—but you never know.

So here I am promising to make this acknowledgments page short and I'm rambling on and on. I'd better stop introducing the acknowledgments and start acknowledging people, or you'll give up before you even read any acknowledgments. So here we go.

Sorry about that. I hope you're not getting angry; I just wanted to clarify things. Do you accept my apology? But how would I know if you did or didn't, right? It's not as if I'm actually here. I wrote this months—maybe years—ago. For all you know, I may have died in the interim. And even if I haven't, how would you tell me you accept my apology? You could write me a letter or e-mail me, I suppose, but that's a lot of effort. Scratch that idea. I'll just hope you've accepted my apology and we can all move on with our lives.

Now what was I doing? I forgot. Oh yeah, acknowledgments. Oh boy. I guess I'll just jump right in. I really was planning to keep this brief; I don't know what happened. So here we go. I'd like to thank:

Elise Glenne, who has learned the art of putting up with me all these years. Well done.

David Charney, my dad. I got all my goofy genes from him. For that I'm grateful. He also happens to be a great dad.

Claire Ackerman, my mom, who let me practice my tricks on her when I was six. She has the patience of Job.

Ken Charney, my brother, who has even more fun with a whoopee cushion than I do.

Bruce Lansky and Christine Zuchora-Walske, my publisher and editor. They saw me through this thing. Plus, if I butter them up, maybe they'll publish another book of mine.

Hank Neimark. He let me bounce a lot of ideas off his head and sent them in directions I didn't think they'd go—like under the couch.

Richard Fusco, because he lent me a book and I promised to include him.

All the comedians and magicians who went before me and inspired me in this work.

Hyram Toggwaddle, Lotta Love, Major Cloudy Spoon, Ima and Ura Hogg, Tackaberry Kumquat, Miranda Pickleface, Primrose Gook, Negative Dimtwit Smith, Pinkey Winkey Foonswoggle, Newton Tooten, James Icenubble, Delicious Berry, Lou Pew, Humperdink Fangboner, Gaston J. Feeblebunny, Mrs. Burpy Knickknack, Cigar Butts, Lavender Yum-Yum Goldstein, Sistine Chapel McDougal, Toto, Shuman the Human, Hogjaw Twaddle, and Lavender Hankey for having such great names.

And you, dear reader, for having the patience and faith in me to read all the way through these acknowledgments.

Contents

Introduction

About This Book

You hold in your grubby little hands *Hocus Jokus,* which is the world's best—and perhaps only—kids' book on how to be a funny magician. I have to assume, therefore, that you're a kid. Look at you…you're just a pip-squeak! You're probably too young to know who Harry Houdini is, aren't you? Huh?

Okay, so maybe you know who Houdini is. But what about David Copperfield?

Oh. You know who he is, too.

Then what about Melvin Fenstermacher?

Aha! Got you there. Actually, Melvin wasn't a magician; he used to drive the milk truck in my neighborhood when I was a kid. But the fact that I remember milk trucks and you don't shows how old I am, and how young you are.

So you want to learn how to perform magic, eh? You turned to one of the greatest magicians who ever lived.

Too bad he wasn't available.

So instead you decided to buy a book. There are many, many magic books out there. They often go deeply into magic techniques like palming, passes, false shuffles, French drops, Spanish drops, and cough drops. (Oops—sorry, that was a bad joke.) Eventually you might want to read these books, but I think you're smart to start with my book.

Just as I've assumed that you're a kid, I'm also going to assume that you know next to nothing about magic. Here's a secret that magicians don't like to tell: You don't *need* to know much to do magic. There are thousands of tricks that take no skill at all.

It does, however, take practice to make a trick entertaining. *Hocus Jokus* is the only magic book that will teach you how to do that. Being entertaining is the real trick to magic. Some magicians, such as Lance Burton (or perhaps your uncle Schloimy), entertain an audience by being extremely charming. Other magicians, such as David Copperfield, are deeply mysterious. And then there's me; I'm just a goofball. That's why my brand of magic is funny magic. (In the business it's often called "comedy magic.")

In this book I'll show you how to be funny. Silly. Amusing. Bizarre. Disgusting. Whatever it takes to keep your audience's attention. Doing a magic trick is like telling a joke. The most important thing to remember is: *Do not be boring!* I can't stress that enough. (Actually, I probably could stress it enough, but then I'd be boring.)

I've already said that there are thousands of tricks that take no skill at all. Well, there are also thousands of tricks that can't be done without gimmicks like thumbtips, shaved decks, cups and balls, Chinese rings, Japanese rings, and telephone rings. (Rats—another bad joke.) You can find these gimmicks in magic shops or make them yourself. I do suggest that you visit a magic shop eventually—they're wonderful places, and I'll talk more about them on page 120—but in this book I've decided to stay away from tricks that need gimmicks. I remember what it was like to be a kid learning to perform magic. It was frustrating when I couldn't try a trick right after reading about it!

Instead, I'll explain how to do simple tricks that amaze and awe folks without a lot of complicated doodads. But before I tell you anything, you must pledge…

The Magician's Promise

Never tell your secrets.

I can't stress this enough. (Okay, okay, I could. But you get my point—and no, I'm not talking about the one on top of my head!) There are four really good reasons for not telling how you do your tricks:

1. Once you tell someone how a trick is done, you can never do that trick again if that person is around. You'll live in constant fear that he or she will spill the beans.

2. Even when people pester you so much that you're sure their lives must depend on knowing your secrets, they're always disappointed once they know. You see, magic tricks look amazing to people who don't know how to do them. But once they find out the secrets, they see how stupid most tricks are. If you tell people your secrets, they'll no longer think you're a great magician; they'll realize you're a schmo just like them.

3. If you tell how a trick is done, you're not just ruining your own show; you're ruining it for other magicians, too. Magic is just a hobby for you, but for many it's a livelihood. If you blab all the secrets, you'll doom career magicians to lives of poverty. David Copperfield will have to

become a dishwasher. Penn and Teller will be reduced to bathroom attendants. All because of your big mouth.

4. If other magicians find out you're telling secrets, they'll beat you up. Of course I'm just kidding. But they might try to saw you in half. Okay, I'm still kidding. They'll make you disappear. Okay, maybe they won't do that either. But they will be really annoyed with you…and I'm not kidding about that.

Now if you're a schmart kid, you might be thinking, "Hey, wait a second, Charney. You're telling secrets in this book!"

You're right. But I'm telling secrets to budding magicians, not to people who are just curious. This is allowed. If you tell a secret to someone who wants to perform your trick, not just know how you did it, it's okay. *Capisce?* (That means "Understand?" in Italian.)

Repeat after me: "I promise I will never tell my magic secrets to anyone but other magicians."

Now that you've made that promise, you're officially a magician, and I can tell you my secrets. Just turn the page to enter the secret, silly world of funny magic….

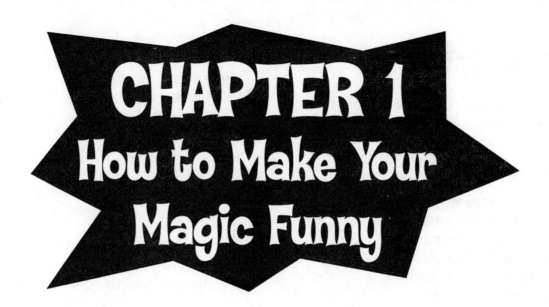

CHAPTER 1
How to Make Your Magic Funny

Hold it!

Before you read any more, know this: You don't have to read the chapters of this book in order. Yes, each chapter builds on the one before it, but I'd hate to bore you. This is your book; you can read it any way you like. Read it upside down. Read every other page or every other sentence. Read only the verbs. Read the whole book backward. It's your call.

Here's a suggestion: Keep reading this chapter; I think you'll like it. But if you get tired of character, style, blah-blah-blah, skip to Chapter 4 and learn a couple of card tricks. Then come back here to read more about being funny. Bored again? Check out the jokes and one-liners in Chapter 3. Or turn to the end of the book and read the index. (Why you'd want to do that I can't imagine—but if you can, go for it!) Then come back again.

That's just a suggestion, of course. You'll probably find my writing so thrilling, so fascinating, so hilarious that you'll want to read straight through from cover to cover.

Well…whatever you do, just make sure you have fun doing it. I don't want everyone talking about how you keeled over from boredom while reading my book and got a big lump on your head and had to be rushed to the hospital and now your parents are suing me.

Character

"Huh?" you say. "Charney, I'm just a kid. I don't know what that means."

What Is It?

Here's an easy way to understand character: What kind of costume did you wear last Halloween? Were you a ghost? A witch? A giant rutabaga? Whatever you pretended to be, that was your character.

Let's say you were a witch. Every time you cackled or pretended to fly on your broom, you were "in character." Every time you asked your friend to trade a Milky Way for a Tootsie Roll, you "broke character."

Being in character means that if you're a witch, you act witchy. If you're a ghost, you act ghosty. If you're a rutabaga, you act rutabaga-y. (Don't worry; I can't pronounce it either.)

Every time you see a movie or a play, you're watching actors who are in character. Actors sometimes study their characters for months before performing.

Look at Snow White's seven dwarfs. Each little fellow has a character, and he's named for that character. What could be simpler? Happy is only happy. Sleepy is only sleepy. Sleepy doesn't get happy. Happy doesn't get sleepy. And Sleazy doesn't get...wait a second...Sleazy? Where'd he come from?

David Copperfield's character is mysterious. He's flirty, too. He often wears a little smile that says, "This is all in fun; don't take me too seriously." He does not pick his nose or sniff his armpits in the middle of a trick. If he did, he would be breaking character and distracting people from his show.

So now you know what the word *character* means to a magician:

A character is the unique person (or giant vegetable) a magician pretends to be while performing.

Your Character

You have many characters inside you already. If you're grumpy when you wake up in the morning, you're showing one character. (You're also acting like another one of the seven dwarfs.) When you torture your brother or sister, you're showing another character. (Let's call that one Bratty.) When you fetch your mom's or dad's slippers, you're...a dog.

Find the part of you that feels comfortable and natural to you and is interesting to others. Present that part of you when you perform—not the part that mumbles, shuffles, and sniffles. Perhaps the character you choose will be simply a part of you that's charming and outgoing. That's enough for a lot of magicians.

If you'd rather pretend to be someone (or something) else, or if you just want to present a more exciting character, go right ahead. For instance, you could perform as the character you were last Halloween. A wizard! A ghost! A size–thirty-two shoe! Or you could make up a new character. Or you could dress up as an interesting person you know. Comedians often do this. They remember people they thought were funny. They dress up as those people, exaggerate their behavior, and—voilà!—you have Eddie Murphy playing a character based on his grandmother in *The Nutty Professor* or Jim Carrey playing a knucklehead in *Dumb and Dumber.* You might want to stop in a costume store and see if it has any inexpensive items you could buy to build your character.

Here are four characters that magicians often use:

✭ Mysterious: A mysterious magician acts as if his or her performance is actually magical. The audience members feel as if they're watching a real wizard. Mysterious magicians sometimes work with fire and dramatic lighting.

✭ Charming: A charming magician is good-natured, smart, confident, and always seems to be having fun. He or she wants love and admiration from the audience (and maybe a teeny bit of envy, too).

✭ Bumbling: A bumbling magician pretends to mess up tricks but eventually gets them right in funny ways. For example, a bumbling magician may say he or she is going to pull a rabbit out of a hat, and instead, out comes a humongous banana. This kind of magician often wears weird clothes. Clown magicians are usually bumblers.

✭ Funny: A funny magician performs a whole show as a big joke. He or she doesn't pretend to be doing real magic. To a funny magician, making people laugh is as important as astounding them with tricks. I'm a funny magician myself, and I stress this type of magic in *Hocus Jokus.*

Don't limit yourself to these four characters. Good magicians create new characters by adding personal touches to these four or by making up their own characters from scratch.

And of course, you can play more than one character in your magic show. I do this. I put on big ears, a seed-corn cap, and overalls and perform as Farmer Brown. Then I change into an eye patch and a red bandanna, disguise my voice (arrgh, mateys), and perform as a pirate. I've performed as a Rastafarian, a woman, a nerd, and a swami all in one show.

Whether you use one character or many, remember that a good character is simple and is easy for an audience to figure out. So...acting like a bumbling clown is good. Acting like a mysterious wizard is good. Even acting like a rude and disgusting goofball is good. But acting like a character who appears every other week on a cartoon that you always watch before everyone else wakes up...well...that's not so good. No one would know who or what you were trying to be!

Building a character can take time. Here are some tips to help you along the way:

✳ Be patient. (Ooh, that reminds me of a joke: A guy rushes into a doctor's office and says, "Doctor, doctor, I'm shrinking!" The doctor says, "You'll have to be a little patient.") The longer you stick with a character, the more you'll think of to do and say as that character.

✳ Get comfortable with your character. Think of lines you can repeat at each performance that will help you stay in character (like *arrgh, mateys*).

✳ Relax! You'll find it a lot easier to stay in character if you just stay loose and have fun. And if you're having fun, chances are the audience will, too!

Style

Now let's talk about style. (Well, I'll talk about it; you read.) What's the difference between character and style?

We'll look at the seven dwarfs again. Sneezy is always sneezing. That's his character. But how he sneezes is his style. Does he hold his hand over his mouth and try to stifle each sneeze? Or does he sneeze with a huge roar? It depends on his style.

David Copperfield's character is charming and mysterious, but his style is the way he flirts with his audience and swaggers around the stage.

Now you know what the word *style* means, too:

Style is how a character behaves.

4

The more time you spend in character, the quicker your character's style will develop. Let's say you've been cast in a performance of *Snow White.* You're playing the part of Happy. As you practice the part, you figure out how Happy shows his happiness. You decide whether Happy wears a goofy grin or a sly smirk. You figure out whether his smile is genuine or is just a way to hide his fear of princesses. You choose whether he gives Snot White—I mean Snow White—a flower or squashes a buttered muffin into her face at breakfast.

The more you play the part of Happy, the more natural Happy's style feels to you. You learn what feels wrong for Happy to do and say as well as what feels right.

Showmanship

Whatever your character and style are, you must have showmanship, too.

"What's that?" you ask. "Show a man a ship?"

Uh-uh. I'm talking about the ability to capture and hold an audience's attention. If a magician has showmanship, no one coughs, no one looks at the clock, no one gets antsy. The audience is spellbound.

Showmanship is how you move, how you relate to your audience. It's your unique personality and your ability to think on your feet. It's anything you do to make your performance dramatic, exciting, or otherwise interesting.

Back to our friend Sneezy. We know what his character is: He's a sneezer. We know his style is how he sneezes. Whether his style is to sneeze quietly or like a nuclear bomb, if he has showmanship, he does it in a way that impresses everyone who hears it. When he sneezes, people may laugh, cry, scream with fright, or be speechless with amazement—but whatever their reaction is, they think, "Sneezy …now that guy can sneeze!"

As a magician, you want people to say something like that about you: "Charlie (or Mergatroyd or Ethel or Myron or Ed…what is your name, anyway?)…now that kid can sneeze!"—I mean, "Now that kid can perform magic!"

If your audience can't get enough of you, if they laugh and cry and are like putty in your hands, chances are you have showmanship.

Showmanship is anything a magician does to keep an audience's attention and interest.

If you don't have showmanship, fear not: It can be learned. That's what this book is about.

Okay, now you understand character, style, and showmanship. But you're going to look pretty stupid standing in front of a crowd dressed as a giant rutabaga with nothing to say. That's why you need some talking tips! And I'm just the guy to give them to you.

Patter

Character and patter are like a ukulele and its strings. One's no good without the other! A character without patter is a mime. Patter without character is just boring.

What Is It?

No, patter is not someone who pats you. So what is it?

Patter is anything you say during a magic trick that makes it more interesting for your audience.

Patter can be:

⭐ An introduction to a trick ("I have here a giant fly swatter—well, actually it's a crocodile swatter—and with it, I'm going to….")

⭐ A story you tell as you perform a trick ("One-armed Louie taught me this difficult sleight of hand. Let me tell you about Louie….")

⭐ Instructions to your audience ("Can everybody please rise and give me a standing ovation?")

⭐ A joke ("A man walks into a restaurant—ouch!—that must have hurt!")

⭐ A one-liner ("You're late; we had you marked absent!")

⭐ Magic words ("Pinky-schminky, alakazoo!")

⭐ A zinger to silence a heckler ("You're dark and handsome. When it's dark, you're handsome.")

⭐ A noise to grab people's attention ("Ahhhhhhhhhhhh!")

⭐ A statement that distracts your audience from something you're doing ("Your fly is open!")

⭐ Anything you say to fill time ("I'm waiting for the President of Swaziland to arrive….")

⭐ A sound effect *(Burp!)*

Patter is the key to successful magic. Performing a magic trick is a lot like telling a joke. A good joke teller can make people laugh even if a joke isn't that great. It's the same with magic. A good magician can entertain people even with really simple or stupid tricks.

Your patter will sound the best if you act confident. Remember that while you're onstage, you own it. Everyone is paying attention to you, and people are assuming that you're cleverer than they are. Use that to help you. Act like you know exactly what you're doing, even if you don't. If you make a mistake, just keep going—and keep talking! Your audience won't know what's supposed to happen and probably won't even realize you've goofed.

Give it all you've got. It's better to ham it up too much than not enough. A good friend of mine always says (after overdoing something), "If it's worth doing, it's worth overdoing." Say the weirdest and funniest things you can think up. Don't be afraid to be a little naughty! A good magician will say anything to keep an audience interested.

Be original. If you see a trick in a book or buy one in a magic shop, use patter to make it your own. If you perform tricks differently from other magicians, you'll earn a reputation for being creative. And if you someday decide to perform magic for a living, you'll get more work than everyone else. More people will come to see you. And you'll feel much better about yourself.

With patter, pretty much anything goes. But there's just one rule you should remember: Your character, style, and patter should match one another. For example, if your character is Sleepy and your style is to yawn all the time, you shouldn't talk about how you love to stay up and watch *The Late Late Show* every night. Keep in mind what your character would say naturally.

On the following pages and sprinkled throughout this book, you'll find many examples of funny patter to get you started.

Introductions

You could start your show by asking, "You wanna see a magic trick?" But wouldn't it be more fun to say, "Did I ever show you my bionic ear?" or "Did you know that I was once kidnapped by a band of roving gypsies?" Questions like these will catch people's interest.

Here are some more attention grabbers to kick off your show:

☀ "This year my mother told me I was finally old enough to learn the family magic trick. It's been passed down through my family for generations. Would you like to see it?"

☀ "I was sitting in a bar the other week having a beer—a root beer—when three guys with pointy hats and star-studded robes came in and sat down next to me...."

✷ "I was visited by an alien from Pluto the other day. When I told the alien that no one would believe what had happened to me, it gave me a magic ball. It said in a strange accent that if anyone doubts me, I should show the ball to prove that there's other life in the universe."

✷ "Did I ever show you the trick I learned from the great Houdini? Not Harry Houdini...Teeny-Weeny Houdini. He was a short guy."

✷ "I was rummaging around in my attic the other day and came across this strange...."

✷ "I was thinking of my college days last week. I graduated in '96. That's 1796... two past lives ago. Anyway, as I was saying...."

Magic Words

I try to avoid magic words like *abracadabra, hocus-pocus,* and *alakazam.* There's a simple reason for this: They stink! They're worn-out. They have no pizzazz. Use these magic words instead:

✰ *Abbykadabby*
✰ *Abracabooger*
✰ *Abracadebra* (This one's great if you have a volunteer named Debra.)
✰ *Abracadoody*
✰ *Abracapocus*
✰ *Abracazebra*
✰ *Alakapocus*
✰ *Boogernose*
✰ *Earwax*
✰ *Epplekedepple* (Then stick out your tongue and give three short raspberries.)
✰ *Have a banana*
✰ *Hokey pokey*
✰ *Hopeless focus*
✰ *Hukus-pukus*
✰ *Mechaleckahi meckahineyho*
✰ *Nov schmozz kepop*
✰ *Onnie swakey mollie pons*
✰ *Poop in your little brother's hair*
✰ *Teeny-weeny Houdini*
✰ *Uncle Fester's big toe*
✰ *Your grandfather's underwear*
✰ *Your grandmother's earwax*
✰ *Your mother's combat boots*

...And so on, ad nauseam. (No, that's not a magic word, though it could be. It means "until you puke.")

You can also design your own magic words. Make up a completely new word or use any common phrase you like, such as *grandpa's smelly underpants.* (That's a common phrase?) The cool thing about magic words is that no matter how silly or stupid they are, they seem to have great power when you say them with a little showmanship while you're doing a magic trick.

Funny Words

When you make up patter to go with your magic tricks, be sure to use lots of funny words. Here are some general examples of boring words you can replace with funny ones:

Boring	Funny
Apple	*Banana*
Ring finger	*Big toe*
Carrot, potato, turnip	*Rutabaga, succotash, guacamole*
Shoulder, neck, back	*Tushy, heinie, rear end, backside*
Venus, Earth	*Pluto, Neptune*
Smith	*Fenstermacher*
Navel	*Bellybutton*
Arm	*Armpit*

Sign, sodium, seven, Sistine Chapel	*Schloimy, schmo, schlemiel, schmutz, schmegeggi, schtick, schmart, schlomozzle*
Reno, Fort Lauderdale, Columbus	*Kalamazoo, Hoboken, Moose Jaw*
Song, dad, unintelligent, procrastinate	*Ditty, daddy, dippy, dilly-dally*

Can you see where I'm going with this? Funny words are words that have unusual sounds *(schlomozzle),* that bring unusual or funny pictures to mind *(Moose Jaw),* or that describe things people don't usually talk about *(armpit).* Every subject has its boring and funny words. Here are some examples of boring and funny transportation words:

Boring	Funny
Boeing 747	*Helicopter*
Bicycle	*Tricycle*
Oldsmobile	*Volkswagen Beetle*
Motorcycle	*Choo-choo train*

And here are some animals:

Boring	Funny
Tyrannosaur	*Hippo*
Rabbit	*Kangaroo*
Snake	*Worm*

And finally, here are some places:

Boring	**Funny**
Garage	*Outhouse*
House	*Doghouse*
Office building	*Igloo*
Tent	*Tepee*
Hall	*Bathroom*
Grocery store	*Sewer*
Den	*Padded cell*

When you're making up patter, throw in funny stories as well as funny words. For instance:

Boring	**Funny**
I was walking down the street when I saw an apple on the ground. I picked it up and put it in my pocket. So there I was walking down the street with this apple in my pocket….	*I was walking down the street when I saw a banana on the ground. I picked it up, but since I didn't have a pocket to put it in, I had to stick it in my ear. So there I was walking down the street with this banana in my ear….*
I often sit at the table staring at my ring finger….	*I often sit at the table staring at my big toe….*
Last night I was at home eating a carrot when a salesman from Reno knocked at my door….	*Last night I was in the bathroom eating guacamole when a two-headed alien from Pluto knocked at my door….*

Notice how I've placed different ideas next to each other in the funny stories. (Who'd have thought the phrases *eating guacamole* and *two-headed alien from Pluto* could ever appear in the same sentence?) You can make even a boring word or idea funny by placing it next to an unlikely partner. For instance, a den is boring—but a den overflowing with succotash isn't. Try it yourself!

Let's see…now you've got character, style, and showmanship. You even have great patter. But you're missing something. I know it's around here someplace. Oh yeah, you need some…

Props

Yup, you need props. So I need to talk about them. Well, I don't really *need* to, but my publisher hinted that if I didn't, he wouldn't publish this book. So here you go.

Oh, are you asking me what a prop is? Okay, I'll tell you:

A prop is any object that helps you perform a magic trick.

Props can be very helpful in making your magic funny. But beware: Props can also be deadly dull if you use them in traditional ways. Be creative when you use magic wands, animals, hats, and other props. Your audience will appreciate your extra effort; I promise!

Magic Wands

The traditional magic wand is a black stick with both ends painted white. You've probably seen a magician in a tuxedo wave a wand like this over some object and produce silks, coins, or a rabbit.

Zzzzzzzzz...what? Oh, sorry, I dozed off. That kind of magic wand is so boring. Don't use it. Use anything but that! How about a magic banana or a magic hot dog? Even a magic toothbrush will do. Just don't use that stupid black stick.

I often use a toy ray gun. In fact, I have a whole collection of ray guns. Each one runs on batteries, has colorful lights, and makes strange noises when I pull the trigger. Whenever I use one, I tell the audience, "This ray gun once appeared on *Star Trek*. It was used by a purple alien with hair growing out of its *pupik* (that's Yiddish for "bellybutton") to turn Spock into a space slug. Now I'm going to use the very same ray gun to..."

Here I can say any number of things: "...make my volunteer's head pop off, revealing a head of cabbage," or "...turn the soda bottle I'm holding into a thermonuclear missile," or whatever.

Here are some other nontraditional magic wands you can try:

* Spatula
* Back scratcher
* Small pool cue
* Limp pickle
* Chicken bone (Tell people it's from a human.)
* Licorice stick
* Anything with googly eyes glued onto it
* Your finger
* Pencil
* Pen
* Stick
* Feather
* Piece of cheese (Okay, maybe that's pushing it a little.)
* Cattle prod
* Battering ram (Maybe I should quit while I'm ahead.)

You might be saying, "Huh? How can I use a spatula as a magic wand? That's just goofy." (Of course it is; this is a book on funny magic!) The trick is to convince your audience that your spatula is magical.

To do that, you need to tell a story about it. For instance, you could pick up the spatula and say, "You think this is an ordinary spatula? It isn't. This spatula was used by the great magician Merlin. He used it to flip magic burgers during the days of King Arthur. Merlin gave it to my great-great-great-great-great-great-great-great-grandfather one day by accident. Well, actually, Merlin was trying to turn my great-great-great-great-great-great-great-great-grandfather into a newt. Things went haywire, and my great-great-great-great-great-great-great-great-grandfather ended up with this spatula. It's really too long a story to go into. But anyway, it was passed down through my family until I happened to inherit it. You will now see me perform some wonderful magic with it. It's also good for flipping burgers."

"Okay," you're probably saying, "anyone could tell a good story about a spatula. But what about a boring old stick?"

Here you go: "This is no ordinary stick. Sure, it looks like a stick, it feels like a stick, and it even smells like a stick. But it's not ordinary. This stick was used by David Copperfield when he was my age. He couldn't afford a real magic wand, so he used this stick instead. Over time it became magical. I bought it from his mother at a yard sale. She didn't know it was magical, so I bargained her down to a buck. She thought she was pulling a fast one on me, but she was wrong. This stick can do wonderful things! For instance, if you throw it anywhere near a dog, the dog will run after it and return it to you. If you hit someone with it, that person will make a loud noise. And then there's this bit of magic I'm about to perform…."

Get it? You can make anything seem magical if you just use your imagination. Stretch your mind. I know you can do it!

Animals

If I see one more rabbit pulled out of a hat or one more dove appearing from a silk handkerchief, I'm going to puke. But that's not the only reason I avoid using live animals in my magic tricks. The main reason is that they're a pain. They're dirty, they die if you don't feed them, and they don't always do what you want them to do.

When I need an animal for a magic trick, I always use a puppet. For example, I have a spider puppet that doesn't fool anyone but makes people laugh by doing goofy things like trying to pick my nose. Rocky Raccoon is a lifelike puppet available at most magic stores. Many stores also sell lifelike mouse or rat finger puppets.

I recommend that you follow my lead and avoid using live animals, too. But if you can't resist, try to use them in unique and funny ways.

Hats

A magician in a tuxedo says, "Abracadabra!" and waves a black-and-white wand over a top hat, making a rabbit appear.

Yucko.

When was the last time you saw someone wear a top hat? Only magicians have them. They don't look funny or even interesting; they look corny. Magic stores usually sell them, but they're way too expensive for a kid like you.

When I need some sort of container for a magic trick, I use a baseball cap or a pail or a box. To make a cardboard box look more interesting, you can paint it or slap some stickers on it.

Although I don't usually use hats for my magic tricks, I do like to wear them when I perform. Hats can be really funny; whenever I find a goofy one, I buy it. One of my hats has a fish going through it; I call it my "o-fish-al" hat. One has two hands on top that clap when I pull a string. Another has antlers coming out the sides; when I put it on, I say, "I always like to put a little moose in my hair during the show." I have jester hats and baseball caps with funny sayings. I also have a hat with a blank sign; I can write whatever I want on the sign, then erase it. In the summer I wear a hat with a gigantic brim or an umbrella hat for shade. Sometimes I wear a propeller beanie or a big yellow turban with a feather and gem. People assume my hats are magical, but I really just wear them to make my tricks interesting and make people laugh.

Silks

Silks are just what they sound like: pieces of cloth made of silk. They can be expensive, but they're worth it. I use them a lot.

I have one silk that folds up so small, it fits inside a thumbtip. The silk looks like a pair of underwear. Another silk I use has a picture on it of a rabbit holding up a sign that reads "The End."

Silks are great because they pack small and play big. In other words: You can fold a silk into a tiny ball, and it looks really cool when you unfold it into a great big piece of cloth. Silks are easy to cart around and easy to hide.

Here's an easy trick you can do with a silk: Tuck a silk in your shirt collar. Cup your left hand in front of your right ear, grab the end of the silk with your right hand, and pretend you're pulling the silk out of your ear. You don't even have to use a silk; you can use a towel, a pair of underwear, or some toilet paper. (I've actually used those things!)

Beautiful Assistants in Tutus

Beautiful assistants in tutus are often boring…unless your beautiful assistant in a tutu is a guy…now that's funny!

Funny Eyeglasses and Other Props

You can buy all kinds of funny eyeglasses in novelty stores. I have X-ray glasses, blinking glasses, and glasses with spring-loaded eyeballs. I have glasses with a big nose, a mustache, and bushy eyebrows. I have a huge pair of glasses with a big nose, a mustache, and bushy eyebrows. I have glasses with a big nose, a mustache, and bushy eyebrows that move up and down when I wind them up.

I'll wear any of these glasses for any number of reasons: to hypnotize a volunteer, to read "invisible" magic words, to help get into character, or just to look goofy while I ask someone to pick a card. Sometimes I put funny glasses on volunteers. I have no shame.

Check out a novelty store, catalog, or web site. Novelty companies offer lots of very silly things besides glasses. Look for funny things you might want to put in your act. For example, I've found a pair of huge ears, a perfume box with a spring-loaded rat in it, a safety pin that appears to go through a person's nose, and giant safety pin that appears to through a person's head.

You can also use everyday objects as funny props. Over the years I've used hand puppets, spatulas, stethoscopes, scissors, underwear, toilet paper, paper bags, rubber snakes, dolls, old toys, and many different kinds of "magic dust." (Anything can serve as magic dust: salt, sand, glitter, confetti—even corn flakes!)

Use your imagination as you build a collection of funny props. And sneak them into your performance whenever you can.

Now You Know

Now you know all about character, style, showmanship, patter, and props. You're well on your way to becoming a funny magician. But wait…in the next chapter there are…there are…I can't remember… what was I going to tell you? Oh, I remember now. Turn to the next page because there are…

CHAPTER 2
Five Important Concepts You Need to Remember

1. Practice

It's important to practice your magic tricks. I'm sorry; maybe you didn't hear me. I'll say it again: It's important to practice! Still didn't hear me? One more time:

It's important to practice!

You probably won't. I didn't when I was your age. Here's what used to happen to me....

I learned a trick. I practiced it a few times. I couldn't wait; I just had to perform it for someone. I usually roped in my mother. I did the trick and messed it up something awful. She saw how it was done. I felt terrible. I promised myself I would practice until I got it right. I practiced a few more times (but not enough to get it right). I tried the trick on a friend and again, I messed it up something awful. My friend saw how it was done and teased me for being such a schmo. I felt even worse. By the time I was able to perform the trick without messing it up, everyone I knew had seen how the trick was done.

Don't let this happen to you! Practice each trick four or five times with no patter in front of a mirror. Then practice it another four or five times. Then some more. When you can perform it smoothly (after about twenty

Practice jokes
Practice talking
Practice in front
of a mirror.
Practice tricks
until I get it
right.
Practice with
cards.

times), start practicing it with patter. Get your patter down so smoothly that you never stumble. You'll get impatient. You'll want to jump the gun. But you'll be sorry if you do!

Now perform your trick for a member of your family. If you mess it up, practice it some more, with special attention to the parts you loused up. Try your trick on another relative. I recommend using your family because relatives usually won't torture you if you make a mistake. (If you have a mean brother or sister, save him or her for last.)

It's hard for people to see their own mistakes. That's why actors have directors, authors have editors, and athletes have coaches. Ask someone you trust to watch your trick and tell you how to make it better. A fellow magician or someone who loves the dramatic arts (acting, singing, and so on) is best.

When you've done your trick perfectly a bunch of times in front of different people, you're ready to go out and perform it for the world.

If you mess up the trick even after you thought you'd perfected it, don't worry. It's not the end of the world—unless you're performing a trick with a nuclear bomb, which is unlikely. After all, it's just a magic trick. Smile and move on to the next one. Then go home and practice some more!

2. Repeating a Trick to the Same Audience

Here's another point I can't stress enough. (All right, Charney, enough stressing already.) I'm begging you— begging you, I say—to show a trick only once to the same audience. If there were a magician's bible, this rule would be on the first page.

When people see a trick for the first time, they don't know what to look for. They're easy to fool. But if you show them the trick again, they watch more closely. They think harder about how the trick is done and often they figure it out.

You may *think* you want to show a trick twice—especially if your friends are bugging you—but believe me, you don't. You have everything to lose and nothing to gain.

There, I said it. The lecture is over.

3. Movement

It's hard to do a magic show without moving. When I first started performing magic, I used a microphone on a stand. (Never mind that microphones didn't exist during the Civil War days.) It was awful. I was forced to stand in one place for the whole show.

Then I bought a wireless mike, and I was like a chicken that had escaped from its coop. Suddenly my show became bigger because I could use the whole stage. Now I can walk from one side to the other to make a point. I can bow, run, sit, walk, swoop, swagger, tickle, dance, or strut. Because my show is bigger, it's also grander.

A magician needs to move while performing for several reasons. Movement helps people understand your character. It also helps you show different emotions. Movement can help you tell a story, stress an important point, or make people laugh. Movement can help you keep control of your show and create stage presence.

Hold it…stage presence? How'd that get in there? And what is it anyway? I'm glad you asked:

Stage presence is the ability to look and feel comfortable onstage.

If you have stage presence, all your movements have purpose. You don't jump around a lot onstage (unless your character is the dwarf Jumpy). You don't call attention to objects or actions you don't want people to notice. Your movements are graceful and natural.

4. Misdirection

You may be thinking, "Please, Charney, it's not Miss Direction; it's *Ms.* Direction." You're not thinking that? Good. If you were, I'd worry about you.

Misdirection is distracting people from objects or actions you don't want them to notice.

Sound familiar? Yup, I just said something like that in the section about movement. Just as you can call attention *to* something with movement, you can also use movement and patter to call attention *away from* something.

Let's say you want to slip a card secretly into your pocket. While doing that with your right hand, you point to the other side of the room with your left hand and yell, "Aaaahhh! A giant bat! Get it away, get it away!" As the audience looks where you're pointing, you do what you gotta do unnoticed. And when they see there's no bat, you say, "Oops, sorry. I guess it was just a fly. But it was a really big one!"

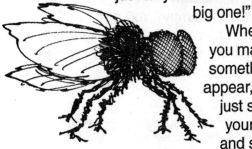

Whenever you make something appear, don't just stick out your hand and say, "Here it is." Pull the object out of an ear, a cup, or a shoe. Create a huge puff of smoke before you show the object, or find it in a giant bowl of Jell-O. Always make the appearance as interesting as possible.

When you need to hide a small object in your pocket, always reach into your pocket for another reason. For example, tell your audience, "I need to sprinkle some wiffle dust on the large crocodile you see before me." As you reach for the wiffle dust, you can drop the object into your pocket.

Always give a reason for your actions. It helps you control what people are thinking about the stuff you do.

5. Testing Your Jokes

How can I be so funny?

I test my jokes. Here's how: I read through joke books. If I find a joke I like, I write it down and memorize it. Then I slip it into my act. If the audience doesn't laugh at it, I ask myself, "Which is the dud—the joke or the audience?" To answer that question, I try the joke again on a different audience. If I get the same response, I try the joke one more time. If I'm still getting a glassy-eyed look from folks after three tries, I give up. I've let some wonderful jokes go. Even if I think a joke is hilarious, if it doesn't work in my act for some reason, there's no point in keeping it.

Lucky you—I've done a lot of testing for you already. And in the next chapter you'll find...

CHAPTER 3
Funny Lines You Can Steal From Me

I have lots of funny lines. (Too bad they're all on my face, eh?) And I'm going to share them with you. I've tested them all on kids and adults, so I know they work in the right situations. Memorize one or two at a time, then find a good place to put each one in your act. When you have those lines down pat, memorize the next few that tickle your fancy and fit your character. Before you know it, you'll have a big collection of one-liners you can say in different situations.

Of course, remember that I've tested these lines on *my* audiences, not yours. You'll need to figure out for yourself which ones fit with your character and style and work for your audiences.

General Silliness

✯ "Now it's time to start the show. If I'm not home in a couple of hours, my mom will rent out my room."

✯ "How many people have never seen me before? Raise your hands. And how many people are seeing me for the first time?"

✯ You: "How old are you?"
He: "Eight."
You: "That's funny; when I was eight, I was the same age as you."

✯ You: "How old are you?"
She: "Forty-two."

You: "Gee, I wonder if I'll be forty-two when I'm the same age as you."

✯ "My fingers never leave my hand."

✯ You: "What's your name?"
He: "Bill."
You: "Hi, I'm Steve. And what's your name?"
She: "Susan."
You: "Hi, I'm still Steve."

✯ "This next trick is done in front of a live audience. You'll have to do until they get here."

✯ "This next trick can be done by any ten-year-old with fifteen years of practice."

✯ "You're late! Do you have a note?"

✯ "I'm glad you showed up. We had you marked absent."

✯ To a short person: "Are you standing in a hole?"

✯ To another short person: "Please stand up—oh, you are!"

✯ "I know *judo, jujitsu, karate,* and fourteen other Japanese words."

✯ "I'm wearing boxer shorts, and I know how to use them."

✯ You: "Where are you from?"
He: "New Jersey."
You: "I'm sorry?"
He: "New Jersey."
You: "No, no, I heard you; I'm just sorry."

✯ "I know a magician who performs this trick without using this hand. I won't let him. It's mine."

✯ "One time I accidentally cut off a boy's ear. I said I was sorry, but I don't think he heard me."

✯ You: "Do you watch a lot of TV?"
She: "Yes."
You: "I can tell; you have square eyeballs."

If the Audience Doesn't Laugh at a Joke

⁎ "Is this an audience or an oil painting?"

⁎ "Is this an audience or a jury?"

⁎ "Who hired this audience?"

⁎ "You can be replaced, you know…by an audience."

⁎ "Ah yes, let's spend a nice, quiet evening together."

⁎ "Is this an audience or a mime convention?"

⁎ You: "Could you give me a number between one and ten?"

The audience members call out various numbers.

You: "Good. I just wanted to make sure you were awake."

⁎ To one person clapping: "Thanks, Mom."

⁎ To one person clapping: "Is that applause, or is someone getting a spanking?"

⁎ To a few people laughing: "Glad to see my family finally got here."

⁎ "We'll have a funeral for that joke tomorrow morning at ten."

Card Trick Comedy

⚹ Invite a volunteer to pick a card. Stick one card out really far from the deck and say, "Here, pick a card—any card at all." If the volunteer avoids the card that's sticking out, try to steer it into his or her hand. It'll be very funny if you struggle. Finally say, "Okay, never mind. Just pick a card." And move on.

⚹ Try to steer a card into a volunteer's hand as I've just described. If the volunteer picks that card, tell what the card is (which you memorized beforehand) and take it back, saying, "Don't pick that card. Here, pick another one." Then move on.

- If a card falls on the floor, look at your palm and say, "I think there's a hole in my hand."

- If a card falls on the floor, mumble, "Stupid gravity."

- Ask a volunteer to shuffle a deck of cards. Then say, "Are they shuffled? Good. Now put them back in the order you found them in."

- Ask a volunteer to shuffle a deck of cards. Then say, "Are they mixed up? Good. So am I."

- Ask a volunteer to shuffle a deck of cards. Then say, "You do that so well, you should get a job at the post office."

- Ask a volunteer, "Would you examine this deck of cards? And while you're doing that, I'll show the audience a trick with *this* deck."

- Fan a deck of cards and say, "Here, take a free sample."

Short Jokes to Fill Time

These are good jokes to use whenever you need to kill a few minutes during a show. Maybe a volunteer is slow getting onstage. Or perhaps the person you've asked to shuffle a deck of cards is doing it at a snail's pace. Or maybe you're waiting for the President of Swaziland to return from the bathroom. Rattle off a few of these so your audience doesn't fall asleep:

- "What's a cow with no legs called? Ground beef."

- "I've been reading the obituaries lately. How come everyone is dying in alphabetical order?"

- "If you don't go to people's funerals, they won't go to yours."

- "My uncle had a seizure at a mime convention. They thought he was heckling them."

* "Why pay a dollar for a bookmark? Why not use the dollar as a book-mark?"

* "Who invented the brush that sits next to the toilet? Man, that thing hurts."

* "My mom thinks I'm too nosy. At least that's what she keeps scribbling in her diary."

* "If I put my hand in one pocket and took out twenty-nine dollars and put my hand in the other pocket and took out thirty-eight dollars, you know what I'd have? Someone else's pants."

* "If I have six oranges in one hand and eight oranges in the other, you know what I'd have? Big hands!"

* "You know why the monkey fell out of the tree? Because it was dead."

* "Why was George Washington buried at Mount Vernon? Because he was dead."

* "You know what they call a man with a bus on his head? Dead."

* "What happens if your arms fall off? You can't pick them up."

* "What did the fish say when it swam into a concrete wall? 'Dam!'"

* "What do you say to a one-legged hitchhiker? 'Hop in.'"

* "You know what a one-eyed deer is called? No ideer."

* "When does a police officer smell? When he or she is on doody."

* "Why do gorillas have big nostrils? They have big fingers."

* "Can anyone tell me the difference between Brussels sprouts and boogers? I'll tell you: Kids won't eat Brussels sprouts."

* "A patient walks into a doctor's office and says, 'Doctor, I'm shrinking!' The doctor says, 'You'll just have to be a little patient.'"

* "An invisible person rushes into a doctor's office. The doctor says, 'I can't see you now.'"

* "I'll tell you why the banana went out with the prune: Because it couldn't find a date."

* "What did the zero say to the eight? 'Nice belt.'"

* "Who invented the first airplane that didn't fly? The Wrong Brothers."

* "You know what rivers help us do? Drown."

* "You know why we buy shoes? Because we can't get them for free."

* "What did Adam say to Eve? 'I wear the plants in this family.'"

* "Do you have holes in your underwear? You don't? Then how do you get your feet in?"

Four Responses to "How Did You Do That?"

1. He: "How did you do that?"
You: "Do you promise not to tell?"
He: "Yes."
You: "I made the same promise."

2. She: "How did you do that?"
You: "Very well."

3. He: "How did you do that?"
You: "Can you keep a secret?"
He: "Yes."
You: "So can I."

4. She: "How did you do that?"
You: "I could tell you, but then I'd have to kill you."

Afterward, to show there are no hard feelings, say, "I can keep secrets. It's just the people I tell them to who can't."

Hecklers

As a magician, sooner or later you'll meet up with people who interrupt your show with questions or complaints or insults. These people are called hecklers.

If it's just the two of you, you can fix the problem easily. You just stop doing magic. It's happened to me more than once: I've found myself doing a card trick for someone who was out to get me or who just wasn't interested. As soon as I saw the person wasn't having fun, I put the cards in my pocket and changed the subject.

If you're standing in front of an audience—especially if you're getting paid—it's a different story. You can't just stop your show. Instead, you need to deal with the problem as quickly as possible. Don't let one person ruin the show for everyone. Usually a few choice putdowns will shut up a heckler. (You'll find a long list of zingers on the following pages.) If they don't work, you'll need to try something else.

It's best not to break character if you can avoid it, but sometimes it's necessary if you've got a determined heckler on your hands. If the heckler is a kid and his or her parent is around, ask the parent to take charge. Or threaten to move the brat to the back of the room.

Here's a strategy that works well for me: I say, "Hello, little girl, is your mother here?" She nods. "Good. Can you point her out to me?" When she points to her mom, I look at the mother and give her a raised eyebrow. This usually encourages a parent to take charge. Sometimes a kid will refuse to point out his or her parent. But then, as if by magic, the heckling stops.

Do whatever is necessary to stay in charge. Trust me: Your audience will silently thank you.

Now for the putdowns. You don't need to remember all of these; just pick four or five favorites. And remember, you should only use putdowns in self-defense. If you use them for any reason except to protect yourself from someone who's being mean to you, then you're the jerk.

"Scram!"

✵ "You're so stupid, it takes you an hour and a half to watch *60 Minutes*."

✵ "You're so ugly, every time you pick up a seashell and hold it to your ear, it tells you to get off the beach."

✵ "You have nice hair… coming from each nostril."

✵ To an adult heckler: "Yeah, I remember when I had my first beer."

✵ "You're so ugly, your parents have to kiss you through a straw."

✵ "You're so ugly, your parents have to tie a lamb chop around your neck just so your dog will play with you."

✵ "The stork that delivered you must have made a crash landing."

✵ "I bet when you were a baby, they used to diaper your face."

✵ "Is it true that when you were born, the doctor spanked your mother?"

✵ "You have a striking face. How many times were you struck there?"

✵ "I heard that you're so ugly, a peeping Tom once threw up on your window."

- "Don't put me down; we're made from the same mold...well, no...actually, you're a lot moldier than I am."

- "Your problem is that you're spoiled ...or does your whole family smell that way?"

- "I heard they were going to put your picture on a stamp. They decided not to because people were starting to spit on the wrong side."

- "You're like an angel fallen from the sky. Too bad you landed on your face."

- "You remind me of the sea. Not because you're wild and romantic. Because you make me sick."

- "Hey, how old were you when your face caught on fire and your father tried to beat it out with an ice pick?"

- "You should let your hair grow...right over your face."

- "You know, you have a chip on your shoulder...or is that your head?"

- "You have a kind face...the kind that makes me sick."

- "Isn't it a shame when cousins marry?"

- "I see Snow White and Dopey had a child."

- "I heard you were a teacher's pet... because your teacher couldn't afford a dog."

- "Hey, is that your nose, or are you eating a banana?"

- "When I look in your eyes, all I see is the back of your head."

- "You're a saint...a Saint Bernard."

- "You should be on a stage...and there's one leaving in ten minutes."

Joke-Telling Tips

- Know your audience. Don't tell dirty jokes to little old ladies in church. (However, they might like to hear those jokes when they're out on their bowling night.) Don't tell silly baby jokes to drunken sailors.

- Surprise is important in humor, so tell the funny part of a joke quickly at the end. Don't muddy the punch line with unnecessary babble.

✳ Some people have a weaker sense of humor than others. These people are known as the humor-impaired or irony-deficient. Pity them, but respect them, too. If someone doesn't laugh at your jokes, don't badger him or her. Just save the jokes for people who can appreciate them. When you're performing magic for the humor-impaired, stress the magic instead of the humor.

✳ Remember that animals don't have a sense of humor. You're wasting your time trying to make a dog laugh. (That smile you see is happiness, not laughter.)

A wise person once said, "Comedy is when you're walking in the city and a fellow across the street falls into a manhole. Tragedy is when you're walking in the city and *you* fall into a manhole." (I'm not sure why I wanted to share that with you, but it seems important.)

CHAPTER 4
Card Tricks

Card tricks are perfect for a budding young magician like you. There are hundreds of great card tricks you can do without much practice. (In this chapter, I'll show you thirteen of them.) Another reason card tricks are so cool is that they don't need any special supplies. You probably have a deck of playing cards lying around at home—and if you don't, you can buy a deck cheaply at just about any drugstore, supermarket, department store, or toy store.

By the way, do you know why the animals on Noah's ark never did card tricks? Because Noah was always standing on the deck! *(Badaboom!)*

Hearts, Diamonds, and Bellybutton Lint

Illusion

You place two cards in the middle of a deck, and the cards rise to the top of the deck.

Props

Deck of cards
Piece of lint

Getting Ready

Remove the eight of diamonds, the seven of hearts, the seven of diamonds, and the eight of hearts from the deck of cards. Put the eight of diamonds and the seven of hearts facedown on top of the facedown deck. Don't let the audience see you do this.

Hold the deck in one hand. Hold the seven of diamonds and the eight of hearts in your other hand.

How to Do This Trick

1. Show the audience the seven of diamonds and the eight of hearts. Don't let them look too long, but don't rush either. In a relaxed, natural way, place both cards in the middle of the deck.

> **"** Exciting discoveries are being made on the frontiers of science. For instance, scientists have just learned that bellybutton lint is magnetic! The two cards I showed you have slivers of iron in them. My bellybutton lint will find these slivers of iron and bring the two cards to the top of the deck. **"**

2. Dig a piece of lint out of your bellybutton or show the audience any old piece of lint and pretend it came from your bellybutton. (I use lint, but you can use anything—a hairball from your cat, earwax, a piece of cheese, perhaps even a booger. If you do use something disgusting, make sure your parents aren't watching. I doubt they'll be thrilled to see you sticking your finger up your nose in public.)

3. Place the lint on top of the deck of cards. Act as if you're struggling to raise the seven of diamonds and the eight of hearts to the top. Then pretend you feel a sudden movement.

❝ Aha! I think it worked! ❞

4. Make a magic gesture or say some magic words. (If you're tempted to use the old cliché *abracadabra,* see the list of funny magic words on page 8.) Then lift the two top cards (the eight of diamonds and the seven of hearts) and show them to the audience. Most people will not remember that the first two cards you showed were the seven of diamonds and the eight of hearts. They'll think the first two cards have risen magically to the top of the deck.

It's amazing how well this trick works. The two pairs of cards look similar, so people simply assume they are the same. It's especially important not to do this trick twice for one audience. The second time they'll watch a lot more carefully.

It's Easy to Cheat at Cards

Illusion

Your uncle Schloimy cuts a deck of cards to four aces.

Props

Deck of cards

Getting Ready

Put the four aces facedown on top of the facedown deck. Don't let anyone see you do this.

How to Do This Trick

" Everyone thinks it's hard to cheat at cards. Nothing could be easier. Any moron can do it. "

1. Hand the deck of cards to your uncle Schloimy. (If he's not available, give them to anyone in the room.)

" How about you? You look like a moron... a strong moron! "

2. Feel your uncle's bicep.

" Please don't hit me; I was just kidding. "

3. Have your uncle cut the deck from left to right into a row of four small stacks. Now the bottom of the deck should be on the left (stack A in the picture) and the top of the deck should be on the right (stack D in the picture).

Four aces on top

A   B   C   D

4. Have your uncle pick up stack A, move the three top cards to the bottom, and deal one card from the top onto each of the three other stacks.

" See? You're a card shark already. "

5. Have your uncle repeat step 4 with stacks B, C, and D.

" Very good. If I were you, I'd get on the next plane to Las Vegas and bet the family fortune. We'll all get rich! **"**

When he's finished with stack D, the three cards dealt onto it from the other stacks will be on the bottom of stack D, and the four aces will be on top of the four stacks.

" As you know, I haven't touched the cards. You cut them into four stacks yourself. Let's see if you cut them properly. I started off by telling you how easy it was to cheat at cards. And look at this—you cheated without even trying! **"**

6. Turn over the top card of each stack to reveal the four aces.

Fancy Moves

The last trick is pretty simple, isn't it? If you want to make it a little more exciting by shuffling and cutting the deck of cards, try these fancy moves.

Riffle Shuffle

To begin the trick, divide the deck in half. Hold one half facedown in each hand.

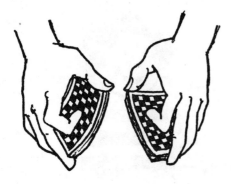

Push the middles of the cards with your index fingers and let go of the edges of the cards with your thumbs so the edges weave together as they fall on the table. Make sure the aces are the last four cards to fall. Push the two halves of the deck back together.

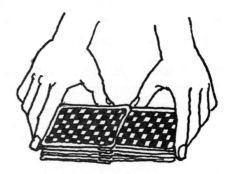

You can do the riffle shuffle as many times as you want, as long as the four aces stay on the top of the deck.

False Cut

With your left hand, place the top half of the deck on the table. With the same hand, place the bottom half of the deck to the left of the top half.

Now pick up the top half (the stack on the right) with your right hand and place it on top of the bottom half (the stack on the left).

At this point you haven't mixed up the cards at all, but your audience will think you have because of all your hand motions.

Reverse Reverse

Illusion

A piece of cheese causes a card to appear at a precise place in the deck.

Props

Deck of cards
Piece of cheese

How to Do This Trick

1. You've been hired to perform at a birthday party. Hand the deck of cards to the birthday kid and ask him or her to shuffle them.

2. When the kid hands the cards back to you, fan them faceup.

> **"** You've shuffled these cards beautifully. Have you ever thought of getting a job at the post office? **"**

3. Glance at the bottom card (the card on the far left) and remember it. (Let's say it's the ace of hearts.) Then close the deck and turn it facedown. The ace of hearts is on top of the facedown deck.

> **"** Crystals are very popular with old hippies, New Agers, and nuts like me. People wear crystals around their necks and put crystals under their pillows because they believe crystals can bring harmony and order to anything they touch. But few people know that crystal isn't the only thing that can do this. Another thing with magical properties is cheese. When cheese is placed on a deck of cards, it will rearrange the cards into perfect harmony. **"**

4. Place a piece of cheese on top of the facedown deck of cards. Put your ear close to the cheese and pretend to listen.

> **"** I can hear the cheese doing its work now. The cards are rearranging themselves as I speak. Okay, I think they're finished. Now we should be able to find any card by spelling its name. Let's check out the ace of hearts. If I deal one card per letter as I spell out

a-c-e-o-f-h-e-a-r-t-s, the ace of hearts should appear as I say the letter **s.** "

5. Remove the cheese and deal one card per letter from the top of the facedown deck as you spell *a-c-e-o-f-h-e-a-r-t-s* out loud. Make sure you deal the cards facedown. Now you have a small stack of eleven cards facedown on the table. And because you reversed the order of the cards as you dealt them, the ace of hearts is at the bottom of the small stack. But keep that to yourself and fib to the audience.

" The ace of hearts is the top card. "

6. Turn the top card of the small stack faceup. It's not the ace of hearts, of course. Turn it facedown again.

" Hmm...I don't know what went wrong. Maybe it's the cheese. The best cheese to use is Limburger. Since we have a holey piece of Swiss, I suppose I should've let it sit a bit longer. "

7. Pick up the small stack and place it back on top of the deck. The ace of hearts

is now the eleventh card in the deck. Place the cheese on top of the deck for a few more seconds.

" Okay, that should do it. "

8. Remove the cheese and offer the deck of cards to the birthday kid.

" Why don't you try this time? Deal one card per letter as you spell out **a-c-e-o-f-h-e-a-r-t-s.** "

9. The last card the kid deals (the eleventh card) is indeed the ace of hearts!

" See? Even ordinary Swiss cheese can do magical things! And the best part about using cheese instead of crystals is that I never go hungry. "

10 Pick up the cheese, offer some to the birthday kid, and eat the rest.

As you practice the "Reverse Reverse" trick, work on fanning the deck of cards and memorizing the bottom one in a relaxed, natural way so the audience won't get suspicious. Also, you'll need to concentrate on the bottom card for a half-second so you can remember it later. I can't tell you how many times I've glanced at a card and then forgotten it. (I can't tell you how many times because I've forgotten that, too!)

To help you perform well no matter what card you're working with, practice memorizing different cards and spelling them out as you deal one card per letter facedown on the table. Each time, place the small stack of cards back on top of the deck and deal them again. Keep practicing until the right card appears nine or ten times in a row.

Sometimes cheese isn't handy, so try making up patter on the spot with different objects. Grab anything—maybe a vacuum cleaner attachment, a banana, a corkscrew, or a Barbie doll's head. If you're using a doll's head, for example, at the end of the trick you could hold up the head and say, "Two heads are better than one." Whatever you grab—and whatever you say—act as if you really believe the object is magical.

The Sensitive Hand

Illusion

You reach into a brown paper bag for a playing card and name it by touch.

Props

Scissors
Brown paper lunch bag
Deck of cards

Getting Ready

Open the paper bag and cut a small hole in the bottom left corner. Fold the bag shut again.

How to Do This Trick

1. Choose a large ape (okay, okay…or a human volunteer) from the audience. Have the volunteer shuffle the deck of cards.

66 While you shuffle those cards, I'd like to tell the audience a little secret: The more you perform magic, the more sensitive your hands become. It's because of all the shuffling, palming, and nose picking magicians do. My hands are so sensitive that if you blindfold me and place them on a mirror, I can tell you what's reflected in the mirror. If I dip my hands in a glass of wine, I can tell you what year the grapes were harvested. If you plug my nose and let me wave my hands through some smoke, I can tell you if it's from a cigarette, a cigar, or your burning house. 99

2. Open the paper bag and turn it upside down to show the audience there's nothing in it. Throughout this trick, make sure the hole in the bag always faces you.

3. Have the volunteer place the deck of cards in the bag, which you are still holding.

66 My, you've shuffled those cards wonderfully. Now could you put them back exactly the way you found them, please? No, no, I was just making a little joke. Please drop the whole deck in this paper bag. Note that I haven't touched the cards; I don't want you to think I've done anything to them. And now, I'll tell you what a card is just by feeling it. Because I don't want you to think I'm sneaking a look into the bag, I'll hold it up high as I reach in and pick a card. 99

4. Raise the bag to eye level, reach into it, and grab a card. Move the card so you can see a corner of it through the hole in the bag. Then tell the audience what the card is.

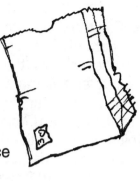

> ❝ Got one. Hmm, let me see...one, two, three...and I'm feeling hearts. This card is the three of hearts! ❞

5. Pull the card out of the bag, show it to the audience, and lay it on the table.

6. Repeat steps 4 and 5 until you can tell the audience is getting bored.

> ❝ I'll do it again. This time I'm feeling a **Q**. A **Q**? What's that? Oh, right...it must be a queen...the queen of spades! Ta-da! Now I'm feeling the seven of diamonds. Yup, there we go! Some ability, huh? ❞

7. Pull the remaining cards out of the bag and crumple it to hide the hole.

> ❝ I don't want to litter, so I'll just put this bag in my pocket. What's this? Did someone put a banana in my pocket? Oh...it's just my pen. ❞

(The joke, of course, is that you're supposed to have sensitive hands and you can't tell the difference between a pen and a banana by touch.)

The Key Card

This may be a good time to tell you about key cards. Using a key card is a clever way of finding a card chosen by a volunteer. Once you know how to use a key card, you can do dozens of tricks.

It's simple: Shuffle a deck of cards facedown and after you do so, secretly peek at the bottom card. (Let's say it's the ace of hearts.) That's the key card. Remember it!

Fan the deck facedown and have a volunteer choose a card and look at it. (Let's say it's the queen of clubs.) The volunteer should not show or tell you what the chosen card is. Close the deck and have the volunteer place the chosen card facedown on top of it. Now the volunteer's card is on top of the deck, and the key card is on the bottom.

Cut the deck. (In other words, divide the deck in half and place the bottom half on top of the other half.) Now the key card (the ace of hearts) is on top of the chosen card (the queen of clubs). No matter how many times you cut the deck, the key card will always be next to the chosen card. You can invite the volunteer to cut the deck, too.

Fan the cards faceup and look for the key card. The chosen card will be to the right of the key card. If the key card is the card on the far right, then the chosen card will be the one on the far left. Now you know what the chosen card is, and you can announce it or make it appear any way you like. Sure, you could just grab it and say, "Is this your card?" But what about style and showmanship? Remember all that stuff I told you in Chapter 1? You're a funny magician, so cough up the chosen card in a funny way. There are lots of fun tricks you can do with a key card—and luckily for you, I know a bunch of them. Here they are….

Twenty-Two Skidoo

Illusion

You find a volunteer's chosen card by repeatedly dividing the deck in half until there's only one card left: the chosen card.

Props

Deck of cards
Feather

How to Do This Trick

1. Invite David Copperfield over and tell him you have a neat trick to show him. (If he's tied up in Las Vegas, get a friend to fill in.)

2. Shuffle the deck of cards facedown and after you do so, secretly peek at the bottom card. (Let's say it's the jack of clubs.) This is the key card. Remember it.

3. Fan the deck facedown and have Mr. C. choose a card.

" Please take a free sample. **"**

4. He should not show or tell you what the chosen card is. (Let's say it's the nine of diamonds.) Close the deck and have him place the chosen card facedown on top of it. Now his card is on top of the deck, and the key card is on the bottom.

" I'll cut the deck a few times so your card is somewhere in the middle, but we won't know where. **"**

5. Cut the deck. (Divide the deck in half and place the bottom half on top of the other half.) Now the key card (the jack of clubs) is on top of the chosen card (the nine of diamonds).

6. Cut the deck a few more times.

" Now I'll find your card. **"**

7. Fan the cards faceup and look for the key card. The chosen card will be to the right of the key card. If the key card is the card on the far right, then the chosen card will be one on the far left.

66 Hmm...it looks like I cut the cards pretty well. Hold on...I'll get it...I'll get it. **99**

8. Starting with the chosen card (that is, counting the chosen card as number one), secretly count twenty-two cards to the left. If there aren't enough cards to the left of the chosen card, continue counting from the far right. Divide the deck between the twenty-second and twenty-third cards. Place the cards in your left hand on top of the cards in your right hand.

Place on top of deck

If the twenty-second card is the one on the far left, just leave the deck as is. In this step you're trying to make sure the chosen card is the twenty-second card from the bottom of the faceup deck.

66 This isn't working. I have a better idea. Have you ever heard of Russian roulette? It's a game where a couple of idiots put a bullet in the chamber of a gun and take turns spinning the chamber, holding the gun up to their heads, and pulling the trigger. The one who gets the bullet loses, and that's it-he or she's dead. Now I may be stupid, but I'm not **that** stupid. So I've come up with a smart version of Russian roulette. It's called magician roulette, and it's played with cards. And here's the best part: No one gets hurt...only tickled! **99**

9. Close the deck and turn it facedown. Deal the entire deck into two piles, dealing to David Copperfield first.

66 As you can see, I'm dealing out the whole deck, so we know your card is in there somewhere. Pick up your pile of cards, please, and tell me if you see your chosen card in it. If you find the card, you get to tickle me with this feather. If you don't find it, I get to tickle you! **99**

10. Hold up the feather as David (you two should be on first-name terms now) looks for the chosen card and doesn't find it.

66 Can't find it, eh? I'll tell you what: I'm such a sport, I'll give you another chance. Set your cards aside, and I'll share mine with you. **99**

11. As David sets his cards aside, pick up yours and deal them all out into two piles, dealing to him first.

> 66 Please pick up the pile I just dealt you and see if your card is in it. Still no go, huh? You should be getting tickled to death right now, but I'm such a nice person, I'll give you another chance. 99

12. Again David sets his cards aside, and you pick up yours and deal them all out into two piles, dealing to David first. He picks up his pile, looks for the chosen card, and doesn't find it.

> 66 Nothing? We'll try it one more time. 99

13. Repeat step 12.

> 66 Your card is still not in that pile? Wow...what are the odds of that? 99

14. Davey (his close friends call him that, you know) sets his cards aside.

15. Now only three cards are left. Deal one card to Davey, then one to yourself, then one to him.

> 66 As you can see, you have two cards and I only have one. I hope for your sake that the card you chose is one of your cards. Take a look. Still not there? I guess that means my card is the one. 99

16. Turn over your card.

> 66 Why, yes it is. And you know what that means, don't you? You get tickled! 99

There's a one-in-a-million chance you'll actually get to perform this trick for David Copperfield. If you do, just don't tickle him for too long. He might get mad and turn you into guacamole!

It's important to practice using a key card for "Twenty-Two Skidoo." There's nothing more embarrassing than going through the whole trick and turning over the wrong card at the end. (Well, I guess going to school in your underwear or peeing in your pants would be more embarrassing...but messing up this trick is still pretty embarrassing.) And besides, you don't want to get tickled, do you?

Practice steps 1 through 7 alone several times, until you feel comfortable with them and can remember the key card every time. As you practice, work on secretly glancing at the bottom card after you shuffle the deck. I often catch a look as I square the deck by tapping its edge on the table. Or I fan the cards faceup after shuffling them and say, "Yup, they look shuffled to me."

It's also important to memorize the chosen card. Every now and then some jerk will try to embarrass you and say you've turned up the wrong card at the end. If it's just the two of you, you can ask the volunteer to write down the name of the card. If there are others in the audience, have the volunteer show them the chosen card before putting it back in the deck.

Another part of this trick that takes a lot of practice is making sure the chosen card is the twenty-second card from the bottom of the faceup deck. First, remember that the chosen card is to the right of the key card, not the left. And second, make sure you count the chosen card as number one when you start counting. Look concerned as you count the cards to yourself. Scrunch your forehead, purse your lips, and shake your head. Don't move your lips as you count.

Finally, when you deal the cards into two piles, keep your pile in order. You can be as sloppy as you want with the volunteer's cards, but if yours get out of order, the trick will bomb.

I Scratch, You Scratch

Illusion

You secretly choose a card from one deck. A volunteer secretly chooses a card from another deck. You discover that you've both chosen the same card.

Props

Towel (optional)
Two decks of cards (with different-colored backs if possible)
Banana
Magic book

Getting Ready

I like to do this trick looking and sounding like a swami. (Sometimes I add a big mustache and glasses. But what do I know?) If you'd like to do the same, wrap a towel around your head so it looks like a turban and practice speaking with an Indian accent.

How to Do This Trick

1. Place both decks of cards and the banana on the table.

66 This trick is called 'I Burp, You Burp.' In order for the trick to work...I have to learn how to do it. **99**

2. Pick up any magic book you have lying around. (Gee, how about this one?) Open it and pretend to read it aloud.

66 Let's see...it says here, 'Never practice your tricks. Reveal the secret after you do each trick. And if the audience doesn't get it the first time, repeat a trick three or four times.' Never mind...that's too much work. **99**

3. Toss the book over your shoulder. (Hmm...maybe you shouldn't use this book after all.)

66 I'll do a different trick instead. It's called 'I Scratch, You Scratch.' You see before me two decks of cards and a banana. The banana is very important. Why? Because it's my lunch, that's why! **99**

4. Toss the banana over your shoulder.

5. Choose a volunteer from the audience and have the volunteer pick up one of the decks of cards.

" Good. Now do everything I do. **"**

6. Clasp your hands together. Scratch your armpit. Pick your nose. See if the volunteer copies you.

> **"** Please shuffle your deck facedown. I'll do the same with mine. **"**

7. After you shuffle, secretly peek at the bottom card of your deck. This is the key card. Remember it.

> **"** Now let's swap decks. No, not swab the decks. That would be mopping a boat. Speaking of boats...What sits on the ocean floor and shakes? A nervous wreck! **"**

8. Trade decks with the volunteer. Ribbon-spread your new deck facedown on the table. (To ribbon-spread the deck, set it on the table and slide the top of the deck to the right to make a row of overlapping cards. The cards should stay in the same order.)

> **"** Spread your cards as I'm doing with mine. **"**

9. Run your finger along the row of cards and take one from the middle. Look at it, but don't show it to anyone. You don't need to remember it.

> **"** Pick a card from your deck. Look at it and remember it, but don't show it to anyone! **"**

(You say this because you don't want to give anyone a reason to see *your* card.)

10. Place your chosen card on top of the card at the far right of your row.

> **"** Place your card on top of your deck, as I'm doing with mine. **"**

11. Close your deck carefully, so the cards stay in the same order. Cut your deck as many times as you like. (For each cut, divide the deck in half and place the bottom half on top of the other half.)

> **"** Close your deck just as I'm doing. Cut your deck as many times as you like. **"**

Now the key card is on top of the volunteer's chosen card.

" To make sure there's no hanky-panky, let's swap decks again. **"**

12. Trade decks with the volunteer.

" Please find your chosen card in your new deck while I do the same. **"**

13. Fan the cards faceup and look for the key card. The chosen card will be to the right of the key card. If the key card is the card on the far right, then the chosen card will be the one on the far left. Grab the volunteer's chosen card and place it facedown on the table. It looks better if you place the card on the table before the volunteer does.

" Place your card facedown on the table. It would be an odd coincidence if the card I chose were different from the one you picked, wouldn't you say? Any magician can find the exact same card you chose, but only a genius like me can find a card that's totally different from the one selected by a sucker—I mean spectator!

Let's see...I shuffled my deck, and you shuffled yours. I scratched my armpit, and you scratched yours. We each chose a card and remembered it. We each cut our deck of cards. Then I placed my card on the table,

and so did you. I'm making a funny noise right now—**burp**—and you're not. Go ahead, make the noise. If you don't do it, I'm not sure the trick will work. **"**

14. Reach for the two cards.

" Look! The cards are totally different! **"**

15. Turn the cards over and reveal that they're the same.

" Oh no! How did that happen? I'm ruined, ruined! **"**

Slaphappy

Illusion

You slap a deck of cards held by a volunteer. All the cards fall to the floor except the volunteer's chosen card.

Props

Deck of cards

How to Do This Trick

1. Your class is having a party. You decide to do a magic trick for them. Look around at your classmates.

> **❝** I need a volunteer... **❞**

Hands go up.

> **❝** ...to come up here and pull down your pants! **❞**

I guarantee this will get a laugh. Now the class knows you're a professional. Of course, you now have to say:

> **❝** I'm just joking. **❞**

If you don't, you'll never get anyone to volunteer again.

2. Now point to your teacher.

> **❝** You look like a good person for this trick. Could you come up here and help me? **❞**

3. Shuffle the deck of cards facedown and after you do so, secretly peek at the bottom card. (Let's say it's the ace of hearts.) This is the key card. Remember it.

4. Fan the deck facedown and hold it out to Mrs. McGillicuddy. (Is that your teacher's name?)

> **❝** Please take a free sample. Now show it to everyone except me. **❞**

5. Close the deck.

> **❝** Put the card back on top, and I'll cut the deck several times. **❞**

6. Cut the deck several times. (For each cut, divide the deck in half and place the bottom half on top of the other half.) Now the key card is on top of your teacher's chosen card.

7. Fan the cards faceup and look for the key card. The chosen card will be to the right of the key card. If the key card is the card on the far right, then the chosen card will be the one on the far left. Secretly move the chosen card to the top of the faceup deck as you look, then say the following:

> **"** Hmm...you did a wonderful job of shuffling. Is this your card? **"**

Hold up a wrong card.

> **"** No? Well, its back looks the same as your card's back. How about this one? **"**

Hold up another wrong card.

> **"** No? I'm going to have to find your card some other way. Let's see...oh, I know! Hold the deck of cards exactly as I'm showing you. **"**

8. Hold out one fist with your knuckles facing to the side. Place the deck of cards facedown between your index and middle fingers. Then hand

the deck to Mrs. McGillicuddy and have her do the same.

> **"** Now squeeze the deck tightly and don't move your fist no matter what I do. **"**

9. Slap the deck hard and fast. All the cards except one will go flying. The card left between Mrs. McGillicuddy's fingers will be the card that was on the bottom of the facedown deck (the ace of hearts, her chosen card). Don't ask me why this happens. It has to do with some scientific principle I know nothing about.

10. Milk this moment for all it's worth.

49

You'll need to practice this trick with another person. As you practice, figure out how tightly the volunteer needs to squeeze the deck of cards and how hard and fast you need to slap it. If you don't slap hard enough, the deck will stay in the volunteer's fist. If you slap too hard, all the cards will go flying.

" Show everybody the card, but don't let me see it and don't say what it is. That card could be any card at all except...the ace of hearts. If it's the ace of hearts, I feel sorry for you. Horrible things will happen. You'll lose all your money and your job as our teacher. You'll grow a big pimple on your nose and you'll be forced to do manual labor. Because— "

11. Now the audience is laughing, since your teacher is indeed showing the ace of hearts.

" Wait a second...that's not the ace of hearts, is it? "

12. Take the card from Mrs. McGillicuddy and look at it.

" Did I mention manual labor? Now you have to pick up all those cards. "

13. Of course, don't let your teacher pick up the cards. That wouldn't be nice. Instead, say:

" That's all right; I'll do it myself—as long as I don't have to clean the erasers later. But can you at least take a bow? I'll take one, too. "

14. As you bow, start picking up the cards.

I have a question. (Actually, I have four questions.) Do kids still bang erasers to clean them? Or is there a machine that does it now? Do you even have chalkboards and erasers in school anymore? Could some kind reader please e-mail me at steve@stevecharney.com and tell me? (Ask an adult if it's okay first.) Thanks.

More Key-Card Tricks

Here are three more ways you can make a chosen card appear by using a key card. Use your imagination to make up your own patter for these tricks. Try to invent your own key-card tricks, too!

Pickpocket

1. Shuffle a deck of cards facedown and after you do so, secretly peek at the bottom card. That's the key card. Remember it.

2. Fan the deck facedown and have someone choose a card and look at it. (Let's say it's the six of diamonds.) The volunteer should not show or tell you what the chosen card is. Close the deck and have him or her place the chosen card facedown on top of it. Now the chosen card is on top of the deck, and the key card is on the bottom.

3. Cut the deck. (Divide the deck in half and place the bottom half on top of the other half.) Now the key card is on top of the chosen card.

4. Fan the cards faceup and look for the key card. The chosen card will be to the right of the key card. If the key card is the card on the far right, then the chosen card will be the one on the far left. Secretly place the chosen card on the bottom of the faceup deck. (You'll need some good patter here to distract the audience.) Close the deck.

5. Put the deck in your pocket. Ask the audience for a number between three and ten. (Let's say the number is five.) Reach into your pocket and pull out five cards one at a time, placing them facedown in a pile on the table. Pull the first four cards off the top of the faceup deck. Pull the fifth card off the bottom of the faceup deck.

6. Turn the fifth card (the chosen card) faceup. To everyone it looks as if you pulled five cards randomly from the deck and magically made the chosen card appear last.

Hat Trick

1. Follow steps 1 through 4 of "Pickpocket."

2. Put the deck of cards in a baseball cap. Hold the cap by its edge, gripping the deck of cards facedown against the inside of the hat. Lift the cap over your head.

3. Tell the audience that the chosen card is the black sheep of the card family and doesn't like to hang out with the others. As you say this, turn the cap over, hold on to the deck, and let only the chosen card fall out.

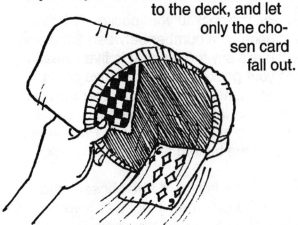

Something on My Mind

1. Follow steps 1 through 4 of "Pickpocket."

2. Hold the deck so it's facing the audience. Slowly raise the deck in front of your face and secretly lick the chosen card (let's say the six of diamonds) as it passes your mouth. (The audience won't see you licking because the deck will be hiding your mouth.) Press the deck against your forehead. Push your hair out of the way if necessary.

3. Say, "I'm concentrating on the chosen card…and…ah yes, I do have a card on my mind."

4. Lift the deck off your forehead, leaving the chosen card behind. It will stick to your forehead because you licked it. Say, "Yes indeed, there's something on my mind…and it's the six of diamonds!"

The Force

A force is just what it sounds like: forcing a volunteer to choose a certain card. The volunteer, however, thinks he or she has free choice. I know eight different forces, but if you can get one under your belt, that's all you'll need. Here are three you can try.

The Cut Force

Place the card you want to force on the bottom of a facedown deck of cards. Place the deck on the table, hand a knife or pair of scissors to a volunteer, and ask the volunteer to cut the deck. After everyone wipes away the tears of laughter, have the volunteer cut the deck by placing the top half of the deck next to the bottom half. Then have the volunteer pick up the bottom half and place it crosswise on top of the other half.

Talk for a few seconds to keep the audience from thinking about what the volunteer has just done. For example, you could say, "This trick was taught to me by Houdini. Not Harry Houdini. This guy was very short—about three feet tall. He was called Teeny-Weeny Houdini."

Tell the volunteer, "Please lift the top half of the deck and look at the card you cut to." The volunteer will seem to be looking at the card he or she cut to, but it's actually the original bottom card of the deck.

This easy force works well as long as you do it only once. If you repeat it for the same audience, they'll soon figure out what you're doing.

The Backslip Force

This is the one I use the most. Place the card you want to force on the top of a facedown deck of cards. Hold the deck facedown in your left hand and grab the top of it with your right hand. Your right fingers should be resting on one short edge, and your right thumb should be resting on the other.

Ask the volunteer to say "stop" as you riffle the deck. Riffle the deck with your right thumb. When the volunteer says "stop," stop riffling and divide the deck where you stopped. Lift the top part of the deck slightly with your right hand as if you were opening a book.

Press the top card in your right hand with the middle, ring, and pinky fingers of your left hand. Lift all the cards in your right hand—except the top card, which will slip down onto the stack in your left hand. If you do this quickly and smoothly, no one will notice the card slipping.

Hold out the stack of cards in your left hand and ask the volunteer to pick up the card he or she cut to. The volunteer will seem to be picking up the card he or she cut to, but it's actually the original top card of the deck.

The Glide Force

Place the card you want to force on the bottom of a facedown deck of cards. Hold the cards facedown in your left hand, with the back of your hand facing up. Your fingers should be holding one long edge, and your thumb should be holding the other.

Ask the volunteer to pick a number between one and ten. (Let's say the

number is eight.) With your left middle and ring fingers, slide the bottom card toward you a little. (The picture shows the deck as if you were looking up at it from the table.)

With your right hand, deal the card that's second from the bottom onto the table. Do this six more times. The eighth time, deal the bottom card. It will look as if it was the eighth card from the bottom of the deck, but it's actually the original bottom card of the deck.

What's Up?

Illusion

You make a chosen card appear on the ceiling.

Props

Tape, glue, or poster putty
Two decks of cards

Getting Ready

Check with an adult (your mom, your landlord, your prison warden) to make sure it's okay to stick stuff on the ceiling. Use tape, glue, or poster putty to stick the back of a card to the ceiling. (Let's say it's the king of spades.)

How to Do This Trick

1. Have your cellmate pick a card.

2. Using the complete deck of cards (not the one that's missing the card you stuck to the ceiling), force the king of spades using any of the forces on pages 53–54.

3. Have your cellmate put the chosen card back in the deck and shuffle it.

4. Pretend you're trying to find the chosen card. Pull out a wrong card and show it to your cellmate.

❝Is this it?❞

5. Repeat step 4 several times, each time acting more and more uncomfortable.

6. Pretend you're finally giving up. Throw the cards up toward the card stuck to the ceiling. Look up as the cards hit the ceiling and fall back down. Your fellow prisoner is sure to look up, too—and see the chosen card stuck to the ceiling!

7. Now go finish the escape tunnel you were digging.

Smart Heart

Illusion

You figure out a volunteer's chosen card by feeling his or her pulse.

Props

Deck of cards
Stethoscope, tongue depressor, or any
    medical prop (optional)

How to Do This Trick

1. Choose a volunteer.

2. Force a card (let's
say the seven of clubs)
using any of the forces
on pages 53–54.

3. Grab the volunteer's
wrist (or ear or nose, or stick your finger
in his or her bellybutton).

> **❝** Did you know that I'm studying to become
> an ear, nose, and bellybutton doctor? By
> feeling when your pulse jumps as I count off
> cards and suits, I can figure out what card
> you chose. **❞**

4. Count up through the cards, starting
with ace.

> **❝** Ace...two...three...four:... **❞**

5. After you say "seven," stop counting
and look deep into the volunteer's eyes.

> **❝** Ah yes...I felt a change in your pulse. Your
> card is a seven, isn't it? **❞**

6. Now call out the suits one at a time.

> **❝** Hearts...spades...clubs...
> diamonds.... Wait a second; let's
> back up. Clubs...clubs...clubs. Yes,
> clubs. Every time I say 'clubs,' your
> pulse jumps. Your card was the
> seven of clubs. Please hold it up
> and show everyone. **❞**

7. If you've got the volunteer by the
ear, nose, or bellybutton, let go and wipe
your hand on his or her shirt.

> **❝** I bet after I send you my bill, your pulse
> will **really** jump! **❞**

More Tricks Using the Force

Following are five more ways you can "find" a forced card. But don't just do what I tell you; use your imagination! There are lots of ways to use forced cards. You can keep forcing the same card and pretend to get more and more upset every time it's chosen. You can tear up a forced card and have one just like it stashed somewhere. You can stick a forced card on a toilet lid so your volunteer sees it when he or she goes to the bathroom. Be as crazy as you can—it'll show people you're a real entertainer and will set you apart from the riffraff.

It's in the Bag

1. Use one complete deck of cards and one card from another deck. (Let's say it's the ace of hearts.)

2. Secretly glue the extra ace to an unwrapped lollipop. Put the lollipop inside a paper bag.

3. Choose a volunteer.

4. Force the ace of hearts using any of the forces on pages 53–54. Have the volunteer show it to everyone but you, then put it back in the deck.

5. Shuffle the deck and toss it in the bag.

6. Tell everyone that you'll find the chosen card without looking in the bag. Reach in and say, "Ooh, there's something sticky in here!" Pull out the lollipop with the extra ace glued to it.

Fingerprints

1. Choose an audience member.

2. Tell him or her that you can figure out what card a person has chosen by looking at the fingerprints left on the card.

3. Inspect the audience member's fingertips and pretend to memorize his or her fingerprints.

4. Force a card using any of the forces on pages 53–54. Have the volunteer show it to everyone but you, then put it back in the deck.

5. Shuffle the deck and fan the cards faceup. Examine them closely.

6. Grab a wrong card and show it to the volunteer. Say, "Fingerprints don't lie. This is definitely...not your card." Put the card back in the deck.

7. Grab the chosen card. Hold it up and peer at it, then say, "Yup, your fingerprints are all over this one."

Peeking Puppet

1. Have someone come up from the audience.

2. Force a card using any of the forces on pages 53–54. Have the volunteer show it to everyone but you.

3. Put a puppet on your hand and have the puppet sneak a peek at the chosen card. Then have the puppet whisper in your ear what the card is.

4. Apologize to the audience for cheating.

Magic Recording

1. Ahead of time, tape-record a minute of music interrupted by someone saying in a deep, booming voice, "The card you chose was [name of the card you want to force]."

2. Tell a friend you've learned a great new card trick.

3. Force a card using any of the forces on pages 53–54.

4. Have your pal put the chosen card back in the deck.

5. Shuffle the deck and fan the cards faceup. Examine them closely.

6. Grab a wrong card and show it to your friend. Do this several times.

7. Pretend to give up trying to find the chosen card. Your friend will think the trick has failed. Ask your pal if he or she would like to hear some music now.

8. Play the recording you made earlier.

Sticky Fingers

1. Find one complete deck of cards and one card from another deck. The extra card should look very similar to the cards in the complete deck.

2. At a restaurant, in school, on the playground, or anywhere you want, secretly place the extra card in a friend's pocket or bag or book or whatever.

3. Force the card that matches the extra card using any of the forces on pages 53–54.

4. Have your friend put the chosen card back in the deck, shuffle the deck, and hand it back to you.

5. Grab a wrong card and show it to your friend. Do this several times.

6. Ask your friend, "You don't still have the card, do you? Could you please check your [pocket, bag, book, or whatever]?"

CHAPTER 5
Mind-Reading Tricks

Some folks believe that people can do magical stuff like mind reading, floating in midair, and bending spoons with brain power. Often they believe it because they've seen it! They've watched with their own eyes as people performed "miracles" for them. Or they've heard about miracles from people they trust.

What these believers may not know is how hard some people will try to fool others. Some con artists spend their lives perfecting their lying and cheating skills. Think about it: If people spend years learning to play the piano, can't they do the same learning how to fool people? They can and they do!

Con artists succeed because people want to believe in magic. If someone wants to believe in mind reading, for example, it's not hard to convince him or her that you're doing it. I'm not saying it is or isn't possible.

But I *am* saying that many of us need to be a lot more doubtful than we are.

Because magicians know how easy it is to fool people, they tend to be doubtful. Magicians like James Randi ("The Amazing Randi") and Harry Houdini made careers out of exposing con artists. Read Randi's and Houdini's books—you'll enjoy the fascinating stories of how they revealed people who'd been fooling the public for years. These people, it turned out, were performing simple magic tricks.

So what's the difference between a con artist and a magician? Con artists lie; they pretend their tricks are real. Magicians entertain; they make sure their audiences understand that their tricks are just for fun. (You *will* tell people your magic is just for fun, won't you?)

Putting your doubts on hold to have fun during a magic show is fine. Being gullible isn't. So don't believe everything you see and hear. And don't believe everything you think either! Lecture over.

The Best Mind-Reading Trick That Ever Existed

Illusion

By reading your mind, a volunteer puts all the red cards in a deck on one pile and all the black cards on another pile without looking at the cards.

Props

Deck of cards

How to Do This Trick

1. Try this trick at a party. Choose a guest to help you.

> **"** Do you believe in mind reading? A sixth sense? How about seven cents? Could you lend me a dime? I shouldn't be joking; after all, this is serious business. I'm about to do an experiment that will show us if, indeed, mind reading is possible. **"**

2. As you talk to the sucker—I mean victim—I mean volunteer, fan the deck of cards so it's facing you. In a relaxed and natural way, arrange the cards as follows: Put all the black cards on the bottom of the faceup deck and all the red cards on the top. With your facial expressions and hand motions, make it look as if you're arranging the cards in a complex order that only you know. Don't let the volunteer see the fronts of the cards.

> **"** I'm arranging these cards in an order that only I know. You will read my mind to find out what that order is! **"**

3. Close the deck and hand it facedown to the volunteer.

> **"** Now lift the cards one by one at a slow, even pace, and without looking at them, decide whether each card is black or red. If it's black, place it to your left on the table in front of you. If it's red, place it to your right. I will be concentrating very hard, thinking about the order of the cards so you can

read my mind and choose correctly. You should concentrate, too, but don't think too hard. Go with your gut feelings. **"**

4. As the volunteer places cards on the table, secretly count the cards while pretending to concentrate very hard. Stop the volunteer after he or she places the twenty-sixth card on the table.

" Okay, stop. You're doing very well. **"**

The top twenty-six cards in the deck were all black, so the volunteer has now placed all the black cards in two piles on the table. But everyone thinks he or she has put black cards in one pile and red cards in the other.

" Scientists have recently learned that the brain is divided into two sides: the right and left. When you're mind-reading, it's important to use both sides for maximum brainpower. This is where the ancient Chinese concepts of yin and yang come in. What am I talking about? I have no idea—but I know it's important for you to do the opposite of what you were doing before. Between you and the two piles you just made, create two more. This time place the black cards on your right and the red cards on your left. **"**

5. The volunteer places the rest of the cards in two more piles on the table. The bottom twenty-six cards in the deck were all red, so he or she has now placed all the red cards in two piles on the table. Once again, everyone thinks he or she has put black cards in one pile and red cards in the other. If the piles were turned faceup, this is what the volunteer would see:

If you want to freak everyone out, at some point during this step grab a card just placed on the "black" pile, turn it faceup, and move it to the "red" pile as you say:

" I'm sorry, this one is red. **"**

6. Although the volunteer has tried to read your mind and separate the deck into black piles and red piles, he or she probably really thinks each pile is just a mishmash of red and black cards.

❝ Let's see how well you've done. **❞**

Tell the volunteer to turn the two piles on his or her left faceup. As he or she does so, you turn over the two piles on the volunteer's right and at the same time, secretly switch them. This is what the volunteer sees now:

The cards are now sorted exactly as they're supposed to be!

This is the best trick I know. I've had people stay up nights trying to figure it out. Some people even believed it was real mind reading! This trick is so good, I almost didn't include it in *Hocus Jokus* because I didn't want to give away the secret. Now the people I've fooled who read about this trick will know how I do it. My reputation as a great mind reader will be kaput. Oh well.

Practice Tip

Step 6 (turning the piles faceup) is the tricky part of this trick. Make sure everyone is looking at the volunteer's piles in amazement before you turn and switch yours. If the volunteer is slow, hand one of the volunteer's piles to him or her and have another guest turn over the other one. Keep your hands on the two piles you're about to switch, so no one grabs them by accident.

While everyone is looking at the volunteer's piles, pick up yours and switch them in a relaxed and natural way—perhaps after straightening them. Don't rush.

Practice this step until you can do it smoothly. If anyone sees you switching the piles, you're done for!

The Wizard

Illusion

A volunteer chooses a card from a deck. You phone a wizard, and the wizard tells the volunteer what the chosen card is.

Props

Deck of cards
Working telephone
(preferably a speakerphone)

Getting Ready

Find a shill. (A shill is a helper who's in on the trick with you.) Let's say your shill's name is Bob. (For years my friend Bob and I performed this trick together. Sometimes he played the wizard; sometimes I did.) Explain the first part of the trick to Bob.

❝ Hey, Bob, want to help me do a magic trick this afternoon? In this trick I'm going to have a volunteer choose a card, then I'll call you on the phone, and you'll tell him or her what the chosen card is. Here's how we'll do it: I'm going to call you around four o'clock, so stay near the phone. Tell everyone in your house that you're expecting a call asking for 'the wizard.' Whoever answers the phone when I ask for the wizard should put you on right away. As soon as you get on the phone, start counting slowly through the playing cards out loud like this: 'Ace...two...three... four...five...six...seven...eight...nine...ten...jack... queen...king.' After you say the right card, I'll interrupt you with, 'Hello, wizard, is that you?' Then you start saying the suits of the cards like this: 'Clubs...hearts...diamonds...spades.' After you say the right suit, I'll interrupt you with, 'I'm going to put someone on the phone. Can you tell my friend what the chosen card is?' Then I'll hand over the phone, and you'll announce the chosen card in a loud, deep, mysterious voice. Then you'll hang up. **❞**

Explain the second part of the trick to Bob.

❝ The volunteer will probably want to do the trick again because it's so cool. We'll do it a different way the second time. This time I'll secretly force the volunteer to pick a certain card: the three of diamonds. Then the volunteer will call you, and you'll announce—in a wizardlike voice, of course—that the chosen card is the three of diamonds. **❞**

How to Do This Trick

1. Some friends are at your house admiring your new motorcycle. (Dream on!) Tell them that before you let them ride it, you want to introduce them to a wizard.

2. Ribbon-spread the deck of cards faceup on the table. (See page 46.) Let one of your friends choose any card he or she wants, and make it clear that your friend has free choice. Be sure to watch what card is chosen and remember it! (Let's say it's the five of hearts.)

" Now we're going to call a colleague of mine-a wizard, in fact-who will magically tell you what your chosen card is. **"**

3. You call Bob. No matter who answers, you say:

" Is the wizard there? **"**

If Bob didn't answer the phone, you wait until he gets on the line. As soon as he picks up the phone, he starts counting through the cards out loud.

" Ace...two...three...four...five... **"**

4. You interrupt.

" Hello, wizard, is that you? **"**

5. Now Bob knows the chosen card is a five and starts saying the suits.

" Clubs...hearts... **"**

6. You interrupt again.

" I'm going to put someone on the phone. Can you tell my friend what the chosen card is? **"**

7. You hand the phone to your friend. If it's a speakerphone, switch on the speaker so everyone can hear. The wizard announces the card in a loud, deep, mysterious voice.

" I am a great wizard! I am all-seeing and all-hearing...and I'm a good cook, too! Your card is...the five of hearts! **"**

8. Everyone screams with delight and wants to do the trick again.

9. Force the three of diamonds using any of the forces on pages 53–54.

10. Offer the telephone to the volunteer. If it's a speakerphone, switch on the speaker.

> ❝You can call the wizard yourself this time. Here, I'll dial the number for you.❞

11. Bob answers the phone.

> ❝This is the great wizard! Why do you keep bugging me? Your card is the three of diamonds!❞

12. Everyone screams with even more delight this time.

The combination of giving the volunteer free choice the first time and forcing a card the second time is what makes this trick work so well. Your audience will never figure out what you're up to!

Practice Tip

In the first part of the trick, as Bob counts through the cards and suits, he should go just slow enough so that when you interrupt, the chosen card will be obvious. And to make sure Bob has the right card in mind, he might want to name the chosen card to you before you hand the phone to the volunteer. If you're using a speakerphone, tell Bob when you're about to switch it on, so he doesn't say anything stupid.

Magician's Choice

Illusion

You correctly predict which of three objects a volunteer will choose.

Props

Two pieces of paper
Marker
Book no one cares about
Scissors
Piece of cardboard
Tape
Large envelope
Toothbrush
Banana
Towel (optional)
Funny glasses (optional)

Getting Ready

On one piece of paper write "In my vast greatness I knew that you would choose this toothbrush! —The Great Stevini". Of course, if your name is Susan, sign your name "The Great Susini". If you're a George, sign your name "The Great Georgini". In other words, put the ending *ini* at the end of your name. This will tell the audience that you're a great magician like Houdini, Slydini, and Linguini. (Actually, that's two great magicians and one tasty pasta.)

Open the book to the first page and write "In my vast greatness I knew that you would choose this book! —The Great Stevini" (or Penelopini, Melvini, or Akbarini).

Cut the cardboard into an arrow shape. On one side of the arrow write "Arrow of Prediction".

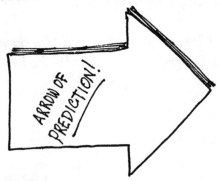

On the other side write "In my vast greatness I knew that you would choose this banana! —The Great Stevini" (or Santa Clausini or Easter Bunnini). Tape the second piece of paper lightly over this prediction.

On the envelope write "Prediction". Put the first piece of paper, the book, the arrow, the toothbrush, and the banana inside it.

How to Do This Trick

1. Take all the objects except the first piece of paper out of the envelope. Place them on the table. Close the envelope and set it aside.

   " A lot of people ask me, 'Hey, if you're such a great magician, can you predict the future?' The answer is 'Yes, I can.' Why, only last night I was in a deep trance, looking into the future. I had my turban and glasses on... "

2. If you like, wrap a towel around your head like a turban and put on some funny glasses.

   " ...and I had a vision of myself in this room with you...and you...and you. "

3. Choose someone from the audience, note his or her appearance, and work that into your patter.

   " Someone in a blue shirt with short hair came onstage and–oh my goodness, it was you! "

4. Look and point at the person you've chosen.

   " In my vision you came onstage and pointed to one of these objects with this arrow of prediction. "

5. Pick up the arrow.

   " I broke my trance and wrote down the object you chose in my vision. Let's see if I predicted right. Please take this arrow... "

6. Hand the arrow to the volunteer.

   " ...and point to one of these three objects. "

7. Gesture toward the toothbrush, the book, and the banana.

8. The volunteer points to one of the three objects.

66 Are you sure that's the one you want? I don't want anyone thinking I've forced you to pick that one. You can change your mind. **99**

9. The volunteer makes a final decision.

66 Okay. I knew you would choose that object because I, the Great Stevini, can see the future! Please read my prediction. **99**

10. If the volunteer chose the book, tell him or her to open it and read your prediction on the first page. If the volunteer chose the banana, have him or her flip the arrow over and lift the paper you taped over your prediction. If the volunteer chose the toothbrush, hand over the envelope and tell him or her to remove the piece of paper and read it. Let the audience examine the envelope to prove that there was only one prediction inside it.

More Magician's Choice

Illusion

You correctly predict which of three objects a volunteer will choose.

Props

Piece of paper
Marker
Any three playing cards or objects (for example, a pickle, a potted cactus, and a baseball)
Scarf with wild pattern on it (optional)
Glass ball (optional)

Getting Ready

On a piece of paper write "In my vast greatness I knew that you would choose this pickle! —The Great Stevini". Of course, if your name is Megan, sign your name "The Great Megini". If you're a Floyd, sign your name "The Great Floydini". In other words, put the ending *ini* at the end of your name. This will signal to the audience that you're a great magician like Houdini, Slydini, and Zucchini. (Actually, those are two great magicians and one delicious vegetable.) Fold the paper and set it aside.

How to Do This Trick

1. Place the pickle, cactus, and baseball on the table.

> **"**A lot of people ask me if I can predict the future. And yes indeed, I can. In fact, just this morning I was looking into my crystal ball. I had my magic babushka on...**"**

2. If you like, put a wild-patterned scarf on your head and tie it under your chin, then pull out a glass ball.

> **"**...and I saw myself in this room with you...and you...and you.**"**

3. Choose someone from the audience, note his or her appearance, and work that into your patter.

> 66 Someone with a blue Mohawk and a nose ring came onstage and—oh my goodness, it was you! 99

4. Look and point at this weird-looking individual (not that you look any better with that funny babushka on your head).

> 66 In my crystal ball you came onstage and pointed to one of these objects. 99

5. Gesture toward the pickle, cactus, and baseball.

> 66 I wrote down the object you chose. Let's see if I predicted right. Please point to one of the objects. 99

6. The punker points to one of the three objects. If he or she chooses the pickle, simply hand over the piece of paper with your prediction written on it and take a bow. If he or she chooses the cactus or baseball, take it away and say:

> 66 Ah, that leaves these two objects. Please pick one. 99

If he or she then chooses the pickle, say:

> 66 Ah, a good choice. Take a look at my prediction. 99

If he or she chooses the other object instead, take it away. That leaves the pickle. Say:

> 66 Ah, I see you've chosen the pickle, just as I knew you would. Please read my prediction. 99

In other words: No matter what the volunteer does, don't take away the pickle—and make it look as if he or she is choosing the pickle. Everyone thinks the volunteer has free choice, but in truth…you're in charge here!

Predicting the Past

Illusion

You predict which of ten different letters a volunteer will choose from a hat.

Props

Hat

Marker

Small note pad or eleven small pieces of paper

How to Do This Trick

1. It's Thanksgiving, and your family is gathered together. Your mom asks you to do a trick. (She's so proud of you!) Get your props together and say:

" Many magicians can see into the future. Big deal. I can see into the past. For instance, I know exactly what I had for breakfast yesterday morning. Some magicians can say when they'll die. Well, I can tell you when I was born. I'm going to show you just how skilled I am at seeing the past. I'll ask this family for ten different letters of the alphabet. I'll write each letter on a piece of paper and drop them all into this hat. The hat, as you can see, is empty. **"**

2. Show the audience the inside and outside of the hat.

" I will then predict the past. **"**

3. Ask your aunt Florence to call out a letter of the alphabet. (Let's say it's *q*.)

" Please give me a letter, Aunt Florence. **Q?** Very good. I'll write **q** on this paper and put it in the hat. **"**

Write *q* on a piece of paper. If you're a neatnik, fold up the paper and place it carefully in the hat. If you're a slob like me, crumple up the paper and carelessly toss it in the hat.

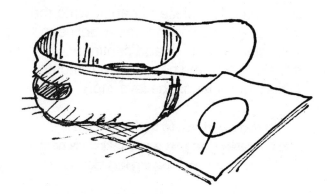

4. Ask your cousin Erwin for a different letter. (Let's say it's *x*.)

> ❝ Please give me a letter, Erwin. Okay, **x** it is. ❞

Pretend to write *x* on a second piece of paper, but write *q* again. Put the paper in the hat.

5. Repeat step 4 eight more times with different members of your family. You now have ten pieces of paper in the hat. Each paper has *q* written on it.

> ❝ We have ten different letters in this hat. Now to predict the past. I will have Uncle Schloimy choose one letter from the hat. Tomorrow when I'm sitting around eating leftover turkey, I will remember clearly which letter was chosen. Amazing, huh? But...wait a second...you'll all have gone home by then. Okay, I'll write down the letter right now. ❞

6. On the last piece of paper, write the letter *q*. (Duh!) Slip the paper between your clenched teeth and continue speaking with the paper in your mouth. (This'll get a laugh; believe me!)

> ❝ I don't want you to think there's any hanky-panky going on, so I'm taking my hands off the paper and keeping it in plain view. ❞

7. Have Uncle Schloimy reach into the hat and pull out one letter. (It's a *q*, of course.)

> ❝ You've chosen that letter over all the others. Please read it out loud. ❞

8. Your uncle reads the letter *q*.

> ❝ Let's see if that's what I wrote. ❞

9. Take the paper out of your mouth and show it to everyone.

> ❝ Aha! **Q.** I knew it. See how skilled I am at seeing the past? ❞

10. Get rid of the papers before anyone can examine them.

You don't necessarily have to ask your family for letters. For example, you could ask for famous names. But beware that it'll take longer to write names, and your family might get bored if you don't write quickly. Or you could ask for numbers between one hundred and one thousand. Be sure to set limits like this so you don't wind up with a first volunteer saying "five hundred eighty-three thousand, two hundred thirty-four" and a second one saying "two." Writing "583,234" while trying to convince your family that you're writing "2" won't be easy. Or how about asking for colors or fruit? Whatever.

You don't have to ask for ten items either. If the trick is moving slowly or your family is getting antsy for some pumpkin pie, keep it to six or seven.

It's important to keep mentioning that you're writing down what everyone is saying. This is misdirection. (For more on misdirection, see page 17–18.) It distracts people from noticing what you're really writing and makes them think you're doing what you say you're doing. It's also important to keep up your misdirection. When all the papers are in the hat, say, "We have ten (or six or seven) different letters (or names or numbers or colors or fruit) in this hat." After a paper is chosen, say, "You chose this letter (or name or number or color or fruit) over all the others." By saying all this stuff, you'll etch into people's brains the idea that all the items written down are different.

I like to use a note pad for this trick. It looks snappy to rip each piece of paper off the pad. It's also more convenient to carry a note pad instead of schlepping a bunch of loose papers.

And I prefer to use a hat for this trick, but you might have trouble finding one that's not too floppy. If you can't find a good hat, just use a small box.

Finally, you don't have to use your family to perform this trick. (Duh again.) Any bunch of people who like a good magic trick will do.

A Very Cool Mind-Reading Trick

Illusion

You read a volunteer's mind and say the color, animal, and country he or she is thinking of.

Props

Zip

Getting Ready

First I'll do this trick with you so you can experience just how cool it is. Don't look at the next page until you've followed all the instructions. Do each step quickly in your head.

1. Think of a number between one and ten. Multiply that number by nine.

6×9=54

2. Add together the digits of your answer. If your answer has only one digit, don't add anything to it.

3. Subtract five from the answer you got in step 2.

4. If a = one, b = two, c = three, and so on, figure out which letter of the alphabet matches the answer you got in step 4.

5. Think of a country that starts with that letter. Think of the last letter of that country's name.

6. Think of an animal that starts with that letter. Think of the last letter of that animal's name.

7. Think of a color that starts with that letter.

8. Now think about the country, animal, and color you came up with all at once, and I will read your mind.

9. Look at the next page.

There are no orange kangaroos in Denmark, you know.

Did I read your mind? If not, you are either a very unusual person or you made a mistake somewhere. I'll explain how this trick works in the instructions that follow.

How to Do This Trick

1. Let's say you want to show how much you love your grandma. Say:

> **"** Grandma, you and I are so close that I can read your mind. Only people who really love each other can do this. I'm going to tell you to do several steps. Do each step quickly in your head. Okay, think of a number between one and ten. Multiply that number by nine. Add together the digits of your answer. If your answer has only one digit, don't add anything to it. **"**

If any number between one and ten is multiplied by nine, the digits of the answer always add up to nine. For example:

$1 \times 9 = 9$ $0 + 9 = 9$

$2 \times 9 = 18$ $1 + 8 = 9$

> **"** Now subtract five. If **a** = one, **b** = two, **c** = three, and so on, figure out which letter

of the alphabet matches the answer you just got. **"**

Grandma's digits should have added up to nine, and then she should have subtracted five and wound up with four. According to the code you've explained, d = four, so she should now be thinking of the letter d.

> **"** Think of a country that starts with that letter. **"**

In English, there are only four countries that start with the letter d: Denmark, Djibouti, Dominican Republic, and Dominica. Most people choose Denmark.

> **"** Think of the last letter of that country's name. Now think of an animal that starts with that letter. **"**

The last letter of *Denmark* is *k*. Most people will think of a kangaroo.

" Think of the last letter of that animal's name. Now think of a color that starts with that letter. **"**

The last letter of *kangaroo* is *o*. Most people will think of the color orange.

" Now think about the country, animal, and color you came up with all at once, and I will read your mind. **"**

2. Pause for a moment and pretend to be reading Grandma's mind. Then say:

" There are no orange kangaroos in Denmark, you know. **"**

3. Grandma will probably be totally blown away by this. She'll think you've really read her mind!

" I could only do that, Grandma, because I love you so much! **"**

CHAPTER 6
Other Tricks

Card tricks and mind-reading tricks are very popular—but don't forget about all the other cool tricks you can do with everyday objects. In this chapter you'll find tricks that use saltshakers, napkins, silverware, rings, rope, string, rubber bands, balls, coins, cups, a banana, and more.

When I go on a trip, I often throw a few of these props (as well as a deck of cards) in a bag and bring them along with me. If I find myself standing in a long line or sitting next to some bored, restless kid at the airport, I go to work. Doing magic tricks is a great way to meet people and break the ice.

Once when I was traveling in India with my pal Bob, our rented car broke down in the Himalayas. We were in a small town in the mountains on the other side of the world, where people rarely saw

foreigners—so everyone wanted to get a look at us. While we waited for our car to be repaired, a crowd gathered. Within minutes we were surrounded by hundreds of townsfolk. What did we do? What do you think? We started performing magic. ("Dental Floss," one of the tricks in this chapter, was an especially big hit.) After a few tricks, the people escorted us to the local bank and into the president's office. The president shut down the bank for a half-hour so all the employees could see our show. And all we had with us were everyday props we had thrown into a bag.

This just goes to show that the Boy Scouts' motto, "Be prepared," is a good idea. And so is mine: "No one beats up the magician."

Assaulted Salt

I can't tell you how many times this trick has come in handy for me. Picture the scene: You're at a restaurant with your family. Everyone's getting antsy because your food hasn't arrived yet. Or maybe you've finished dinner and you're waiting for Aunt Zelda to return from the bathroom. It's time for a trick!

Illusion

You whack a saltshaker, and it passes right through the table.

Props

Coin
Saltshaker with a flat or rounded top
Paper napkin

Getting Ready

Make sure you've got the right kind of props on hand. If you're at a fancy restaurant, the saltshakers may have pointy tops, and the napkins may be cloth—in which case you're out of luck. If you're at a diner with cheap saltshakers and paper napkins, you're on easy street.

How to Do This Trick

1. Place the coin on the table and get your family's attention.

> " Wanna see me defy the laws of physics? I can make this coin pass right through the table. "

2. Wrap the saltshaker tightly in the napkin. Place the wrapped shaker on top of the coin. Keep holding the shaker with one hand.

3. Say the following magic words:

> " Aunt Zelda's underwear! "

(If Aunt Zelda is taking a long time in the bathroom, this is sure to get a good laugh.) Then hit the top of the shaker with your other hand.

4. Lift the wrapped shaker and hold it over your lap as you look to see if the coin is gone. It's not, of course.

> **"** Maybe I used the wrong magic words. I better try it again. **"**

5. Place the wrapped shaker on top of the coin again. This time cry:

> **"** Aunt Zelda's nose hair! **"**

Then whack the top of the shaker.

6. Once again lift the wrapped shaker and hold it over your lap as you look to see if the coin is gone. It's still there.

> **"** That's odd...nose hair usually does the trick. I'm going to have to use some really powerful magic words this time. **"**

As you talk, secretly drop the shaker into your lap. Keep holding the napkin as if the shaker is still inside it. Because the napkin was wrapped tightly around the shaker, it will keep the saltshaker's shape. (Hey, a tongue twister!)

7. Place the shaker-shaped napkin on top of the coin. Shout:

> **"** Aunt Zelda's earwax! **"**

Then smack the napkin. As it collapses, spread your legs and let the salt-shaker drop onto the floor.

8. Lift the napkin and look for the coin. It's still there, but the shaker's not—it seems to have passed right through the table!

9. As everyone looks at you in awe, pick up the saltshaker so your server doesn't have to do it. You can all leave when Aunt Zelda finally comes back with toilet paper stuck to her shoe.

Practice Tip

Make sure the napkin will cover the saltshaker completely and hold its shape. Don't wrap the napkin so tightly that it tears. When you move the shaker over your lap, do it in a relaxed and natural way. Stare at the coin as you do so to keep the audience focused on the coin.

The Magnetic Hand

This trick, like the last one, is perfect for the dinner table.

Illusion

A knife magnetically sticks to the palm of your hand.

Props

Butter knife

Getting Ready

This trick works best if you're wearing long sleeves.

How to Do This Trick

" I've recently discovered that I can create an incredible amount of static electricity with my hand–so much that my hand becomes magnetic. To prove it, I'll make a knife stick to my palm. "

1. Rub your right hand hard on something funny, like your uncle Malachi's bald head or your little brother's tush.

" My right hand is now a powerful magnet. "

2. Pick up something metal with your right hand. Pretend the object is strongly attracted to your hand. Struggle to pull the object off your hand, then finally pretend to succeed.

3. Hold out your right hand, palm-up. Pick up the knife with your left hand and lay it across your right palm. Grab your right wrist with your left hand.

4. Turn your right palm away from the audience. As you do so, secretly extend the index finger of your left hand and with it press the knife against your right palm. Because your palm is facing away from the audience, they can't see that your left index finger is holding the knife in place. To them it looks as if the knife is stuck to your hand magnetically. Long sleeves will help prevent the audience from noticing that one of your left fingers isn't visible.

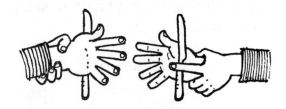

5. Keep holding the knife with your left index finger and shake your right hand, pretending you're trying to get rid of the knife. The knife stays put, of course.

6. Turn your right hand back to its original position (palm-up). When you've turned your hand just far enough so the knife won't fall but the audience still can't see your left index finger, release the knife, move your finger back to its original position (grasping your right wrist), and show the audience that nothing is holding the knife in place. Then say:

> **"** Static electricity works only for a little while. **"**

7. Turn your palm over and let the knife fall onto the table. Be careful not to break any dishes!

More Magnetism

Illusion

A knife magnetically sticks to your laced fingers.

Props

Butter knife

How to Do This Trick

" Recently while shaking hands with David Blaine, I gave him quite a shock. That's how I discovered that I can create an incredible amount of static electricity with my hands—so much that they become magnetic. To prove it, I'll rub my hands together, then make a knife cling to my fingers. **"**

1. Rub your hands together hard.

" My hands are now powerful magnets. **"**

2. Pick up something metal. Pretend that the object is strongly attracted to your hand. Struggle to pull the object off your hand for a while, then finally pretend to succeed.

3. Place the knife on the table so its handle extends beyond the edge.

4. Put your hands in your lap (palms facing you) so your left and right fingers are extended toward each other. Curl your ring fingers.

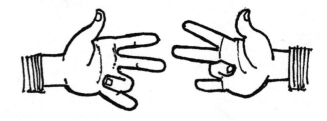

5. Lace your extended fingers together while keeping your ring fingers curled. Lift your hands and hold them under the knife handle. Your thumbs should be level with the tabletop, and your fingers should be below the tabletop, where the audience can't see them. Grasp the knife with your thumbs near the top of the handle. Lift the knife off the table with your thumbs. As you do so, curl your ring fingers around the knife handle. The handle is now hidden from the audience's view by your laced fingers.

6. Move your thumbs away from the knife.

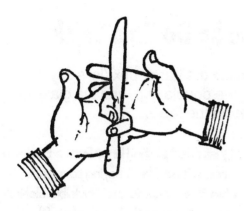

To the audience, it looks as if the knife is stuck magnetically to your laced fingers.

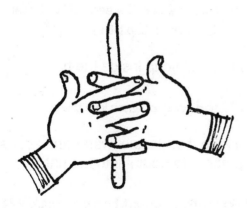

7. After holding the knife this way for a few seconds, grab the blade with your thumbs and separate your hands.

Hatful of Water

Illusion

You pour a glass of water into an empty hat. Then you put an empty paper cup in the hat. When you take out the cup, it's full of water. The hat is dry and empty.

Props

Hat or box
Scissors
Two paper cups with rims
Glass of water

Getting Ready

If you use a hat for this trick, make sure it's a sturdy one. A flimsy or floppy hat won't work.

Carefully cut the rim off one cup and cut the bottom out of the other cup. Tuck the bottomless cup inside the rimless one so together, they look like one cup.

RIM CUT OFF
A
B
BOTTOM CUT OUT
CUP B INSIDE CUP A

How to Do This Trick

1. Place the hat or box (let's say it's a hat), the double cup, and the glass of water on the table.

> **"** I just read all the Harry Potter books in one sitting. I kept saying to myself, 'Oh, big deal—I can do that.' Invisible cloaks? Magic wands? That's kid stuff. For instance, here's a trick they teach at Hogwarts—I can do it just as well as Harry. I have a glass of water, an empty hat, and a cup. I think it was in the second book that Harry put a cup into a hat... **"**

Put the double cup inside the hat.

> **"** ...and poured water into the cup. **"**

2. Pick up the glass of water and act as if you're about to pour it into the hat.

> **"** No, no—that wouldn't be magic, would it? I know: The cup didn't go into the hat; the hat went into the cup! **"**

3. Set down the glass of water. With one hand, secretly separate the cups inside the hat. Then lift out the bottomless one, leaving the rimless one in the hat. The audience can't see in the hat, and they don't know there are two cups, so they think you've removed the only cup. Keep the hat and the cup at the audience's eye level.

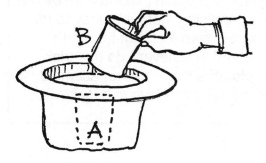

> **"** Maybe it was in the third book... they all sort of blend together. Anyway, Harry put the hat in the cup and the water in the– **"**

4. Try to put the hat inside the cup. It won't fit.

> **"** No, wait...that's not right. I know: The glass goes in the hat, and the cup goes in the–no, no, still wrong. Maybe it was the fourth book. Oh, I've got it! The water goes in the hat! **"**

5. Pour the water into the rimless cup inside the hat. The audience doesn't know the cup is in there, so they think you're pouring the water straight into the hat. Scrunch up your face as if you've just made a mistake.

> **"** Uh-oh. I think I goofed. **"**

6. Slip the bottomless cup back inside the rimless cup. You now have a double cup full of water inside the hat. The audience, of course, thinks you've just put the only cup there is inside a wet hat.

> **"** Oh boy. I really messed up. I guess Harry Potter is a better wizard than me after all. **"**

7. Take the double cup out of the hat and pour the water back into the glass.

" Maybe I'd better read those books again. This is very embarrassing. "

8. Take a drink of water from the glass. Everyone is amazed. They think you made a puddle of water in the hat magically leap into the cup. And you're acting as if you haven't done a darn thing!

Practice Tip

Alas, this is one trick you'll have to practice a lot. It has many details you need to memorize. And like a dance, it works only when all the steps are perfect. If you don't spend a lot of time practicing them, it's easy to trip over your own feet. But it's worth the effort! Whenever I do this trick, people always gasp in amazement. Let me tell you: I love this trick!

And the Dish Ran Away with the Glass

Illusion

You balance a drinking glass on the rim of a dinner plate.

Props

Dinner plate
Drinking glass

How to Do This Trick

" You know, I wasn't always the poor slob I am today. I used to be a tightrope walker! It took years to learn. My teacher first made me practice balancing objects on each other. I spent weeks learning to balance a banana on a jellybean. Then I balanced Jell-O on a corkscrew. Man, that was hard. But I did it. One of the easier tasks my teacher gave me was to balance a glass on the rim of a plate. I wonder if I can still do it. Do you mind if I try? **"**

1. Hold the plate upright with your right hand. Your fingers should grasp the rim at the two o'clock position.

2. Place the glass on the top of the rim of the plate with your left hand, then let go of the glass. It will fall off. Be ready to catch it.

" Hmm...I guess I'm out of practice. I'll try it again. **"**

3. Try again. You fail again.

4. Try once more. This time as you place the glass on the rim, use your right thumb to help balance it. The audience won't see your thumb because the plate is hiding it. Keep your fingers still so the audience won't suspect any movement behind the plate.

" My teacher was right: It's like riding a bike! You pick it up again in no time. Maybe I should drop out of school and go back to tightrope walking. **"**

5. After balancing the glass for about five seconds, lift it with your left hand. Set the glass and plate on the table.

I'm Rich, I Tell You, Rich!

Illusion

An endless supply of quarters appears from anywhere you want.

Props

Scissors
Paper cup
About eight quarters

Getting Ready

Cut a small slit at the bottom of the side of the cup. The slit should be just big enough for a quarter to slip through.

How to Do This Trick

1. Hold the cup in your right hand, with your thumb on the rim and your fingers underneath the cup. Make sure the slit is facing you. Drop quarters into the cup as you say:

" A lot of people think I do magic shows for nothing. Ha! I get paid big bucks for this. In fact, I was told that someone in this audience has the rest of my money. Is it you? **"**

2. Point to an audience member.

" What's your name? Aha! I was told that you had the rest of my money. Hand it over. **"**

Your victim has no idea what you're talking about. Have him or her stand up.

" Wait a second; what's that behind your ear? **"**

3. Tilt the cup toward you so a quarter secretly slips through the slit and into your palm.

Grab the cup with your left hand and hold it with your thumb on the rim and your fingers underneath the cup. Don't let the audience see the quarter in your right hand.

4. With your right hand, pretend to pull a quarter from behind your victim's left ear. Drop the quarter into the cup.

❝And here's one behind the other ear.❞

5. Repeat step 3 using the opposite hands. With your left hand, pretend to pull a quarter from behind your victim's right ear. Drop the quarter into the cup.

❝Hmm...you weren't going to give me this money, were you? You were going to use it to buy candy.❞

6. Repeat step 3. With your right hand, pretend to pull a quarter from your victim's hair. Drop the quarter into the cup.

❝Lift your arm, please. Aha–here's one in your armpit. You'll do anything to keep this money from me!❞

7. Repeat step 3 using the opposite hands. With your left hand, pretend to pull a quarter from your victim's right armpit. Drop the quarter into the cup.

❝Lift your other arm. Here's another quarter in your other armpit.❞

8. Repeat step 3. With your right hand, pretend to pull a quarter from your victim's left armpit. Drop the quarter into the cup.

9. Show the audience the bottom of the cup, tapping it with one of the quarters to prove it's solid. Remember to keep the slit hidden!

    " Here's one in your tush! You should be ashamed of yourself. **"**

10. Repeat step 3 using the opposite hands. With your left hand, pretend to pull a quarter from your victim's rear end. Drop the quarter into the cup and scold your victim:

    " Next time you have money for me, you better hand it over. But to show you how

forgiving I am, I'm going to give you one of my quarters to keep. **"**

11. Give your victim a quarter.

    " Now have a seat. I hope you've learned your lesson. **"**

12. Pour the quarters into your hand and crush the cup to hide the slit. As you do this, say:

    " I'm rich, I tell you, rich! **"**

Practice getting quarters through the slit and switching the cup from hand to hand until you can do both effortlessly.

If you have trouble getting a quarter through the slit, jingle the quarters until one slips through. The audience will think you're just measuring how many quarters you've collected in the cup. I find that if I jerk the cup forward slightly, a quarter often slips backward through the slit and into my palm. If you try this trick, don't jerk the cup too hard, or your audience will wonder what you're up to.

Also practice palming the quarter (keeping it hidden in the palm of your hand). Move your hand naturally as you reach over and pretend to pull a quarter from someone's ear, nose, tush, or whatever.

Be creative as you make quarters appear. You can pull them from other people's bodies, from your own ears, or from your dog's behind (if you can get Fido to stay still long enough). When I'm planning to pull a quarter from some-one's hair, I like to drop the coin into the person's hair and then take my time looking for it. It adds to the drama.

You can, of course, keep "finding" quarters forever, but I don't recommend it. When your audience falls asleep or you get bored, it's time to stop.

Practice this entire trick in front of a mirror until you get it right.

Dental Floss

Illusion

You magically make two pieces of rope become one. Then you cut the rope in two again with your bare fingers and make the ropes grow longer and shorter.

Props

Six-inch piece of rope
Four-foot piece of rope

Choose rope that's about the thickness of a clothesline. You can use any kind of rope, but the best is unbleached cotton. Magic shops sell it in fifty-foot lengths. You might also find it at a hardware store. I once bought some cheapo rope at a hardware store. It was plastic in the middle with cotton on the outside. I pulled out the plastic and wound up with a nice soft cotton rope.

Getting Ready

Hold both ends of the short rope between your left index finger and thumb. Thread the long rope through the loop you've just made and let its ends hang down. Adjust the long rope so the right end hangs about four inches lower than the left end. Make sure you're holding the ropes at the spot where they're linked. This will hide the link from the audience. Hold your hand so your knuckles are facing the audience and your palm is facing you. The audience will think you're holding two pieces of rope, each about two feet in length.

How to Do This Trick

“ The first magic trick I ever did was with a piece of dental floss. Let me tell you the story. How many of you have brothers or sisters? I have a younger brother. In my house, if a piece of pie is cut in two and my brother gets even one more molecule than me, I yell, 'Mom, he got a bigger piece than me!' And of course if I get the bigger piece, he complains. This doesn't happen only with pie. We argue over everything—even liver!

Well, one night my mother was watching TV, and she came in during a commercial to give my brother and me our dental floss. She gave me this piece... **"**

1. Point to the lower end of the long rope.

" ...and she gave my brother this piece. **"**

2. Point to the higher end of the long rope.

" You know what he yelled, right? **'Mom, he got a bigger piece than me!'** She took the floss away from us and started over again. **"**

3. With your right hand, grab the right end of the long rope (the end that's hanging lower) and lift it next to the right end of the short rope.

4. Hold these two ends in your right palm so the audience can't see them. Pull your hands apart, and as you do so,

release the short rope from your left hand so it winds up between your right thumb and index finger. At the same time, let the right end of the long rope slide from between your right thumb and index finger so it winds up between your right pinky finger and palm. Because the gap between the two ropes is hidden by your hand, the audience will think you've magically joined them into one long rope.

" My mom said if she tied the two ends of the floss together and cut opposite the knot, we'd get two equal pieces. **"**

5. Cross the free ends of both ropes. Keep holding the hidden ends in your right hand. To the audience members, who think you're holding one long rope, it looks as if you've looped the rope.

6. Pretend to tie the crossed ends together. First loop the short rope under the free end of the long rope. Hold both ends of the short rope in your left hand and keep both ends of the long rope hidden in your right hand. Now knot the short rope around the long rope. Keep

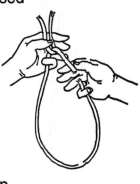

both ends of the long rope hidden in your right hand. The audience thinks you've simply tied the ends of one long rope together.

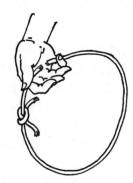

66 My mom heard the commercial ending, and she didn't have time to find a pair of scissors. So she just snipped the floss with her fingers. **99**

7. "Cut" the long rope opposite the knot by moving your left index and middle fingers like a pair of scissors. As you do so, drop the end of the long rope that doesn't have the short rope tied to it. The audience thinks you've magically cut the rope with your bare fingers.

8. Carefully untie the short rope, but keep it looped around the long rope so you're holding the ropes the same way you were at the beginning of this trick. (See "Getting Ready," page 94.) The only difference is that the right end of the long rope is only hanging a few inches below

96

your hand. To the audience, it looks as if you're holding a really long rope and a really short one.

66 My mom then untied the floss. She gave me this long piece... **99**

9. Point to the lower (left) end of the long rope.

66 ...and she gave my brother this little shrimpy piece. **99**

10. Point to the higher (right) end of the long rope.

66 You know what he yelled, right? 'Mom, he got a **bigger piece than me!**' My mom's TV show was coming back on, and she was missing it—so she grabbed that shrimpy piece of floss and stretched and stretched and stretched it until it was as long as the other one. **99**

11. Pull the higher (right) end of the long rope until it's even with the other end.

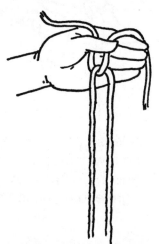

"She gave my brother one piece and gave me the other. Then she made a big mistake. She left the room. Just to bug my brother, as soon as she left, I snatched his piece of floss and tied it to mine."

12. Knot the short rope around the long one. The audience will think you've tied two equal-length ropes together. Hold one end of the long rope with your right hand and let the other end dangle. The knot will be in the middle of the long rope.

13. Grab the dangling end of the long rope with your left hand. Move your right hand so it's holding the rope lightly next to your left hand. Wrap the rope around your left hand as you let the rope slide through your right hand. When the knot slides into your right hand, grab it and keep it in your hand as you keep winding. The knot will be dragged to the end of the rope. As you finish winding the rope around your left hand, the knot will slip off into your right hand. Hold the end

of the rope with your right hand and keep the knot hidden in it.

"I started flossing. You know what my brother yelled, right? **'Mom, he took my dental floss!'** She came running in and asked, 'Steve, did you take his dental floss?' I said, 'No, Mom, I just have one piece.' She said, 'Let me see that floss. If it turns out to be two pieces tied together, you're in big trouble.' I said, 'Honest, Mom, it's just one piece.' And that's how I escaped a spanking."

14. Slowly unwind the rope from your left hand and show the audience that it's just one rope. The knotted short rope is still hidden in your right hand. With your left hand, give the long rope to the audience so they can examine it. If you like, secretly stuff the knot into your pocket to get rid of the evidence of hanky-panky.

Jumping Rubber Band

This trick is perfect for when you find yourself in a room with some rubber bands and bored people.

Illusion

A rubber band magically jumps from one pair of fingers to another.

Props

Two rubber bands, each about the same width as your hand

How to Do This Trick

" One great thing about being a magician is that if I'm ever sent to prison, I could escape over the wall in a snap—even if it's topped with barbed wire. Let me show you. "

1. Place one rubber band around your index and middle fingers. Twist the other rubber band around the tops of all four fingers. (To do this, loop the rubber band around one finger. Twist it once, then loop it around the next finger. Keep going until all four fingers are looped.)

" Let's say my hand is the prison wall. On the top of the wall is barbed wire. "

2. Point to the twisted rubber band.

" This rubber band is me. "

3. Point to the other rubber band.

4. Show your pals that you can't take the first rubber band off your fingers without removing the second one. Show that the first rubber band is wrapped around only the first two fingers by holding your hand palm-up with your fingers extended and snapping the rubber band on the palm side of your hand.

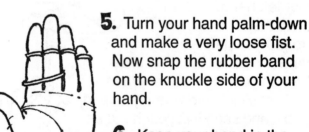

5. Turn your hand palm-down and make a very loose fist. Now snap the rubber band on the knuckle side of your hand.

6. Keep your hand in the same position and snap the rubber band on the palm side again. As you stretch the rubber band, curl all four of your fingertips inside it. When you let go

of the rubber band, it will extend across all four fingertips. But your audience will see only the back of your hand with the rubber band still encircling your index and middle fingers.

" To jump over the wall, all I have to do is this. "

7. Say a few magic words and open your hand quickly, keeping it palm-down. The rubber band jumps over to your ring and pinky fingers.

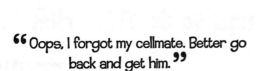

" Oops, I forgot my cellmate. Better go back and get him. "

8. Repeat steps 6 and 7 to return the rubber band to its original position.

" Oh, he's been paroled already. I'll escape again. "

9. Repeat steps 6 and 7. Continue doing so as many times as you like.

" Wait, I forgot my toothbrush. I better go back and get it.... Now I can escape one more time.... What about my teddy bear? Over the wall again.... Hey, this is fun! I hope the guards don't shoot me. "

10. Keep it up until your friends threaten to throw you in prison for real.

Pluto's Ball

This is one of the coolest tricks I know. People are totally blown away by it—and it's so easy!

Illusion

A ball disappears from under a cloth, then reappears.

Props

Small foam ball, large coin, or any object you can palm easily
Piece of cloth big enough to cover your hand

Getting Ready

Find a shill. (A shill is a helper who's in on the trick with you.) Explain the trick to your shill.

66 Want to help me do a magic trick? I'm going to make a ball disappear from under a cloth, then make it reappear. Here's how it'll work: I'll hold the ball in my hand and cover it with the cloth. I'll ask everyone in the room to feel under the cloth and make sure the ball is there. You'll be the last person to feel under the cloth. As you do so, you'll secretly take the ball from my hand. Then I'll lift the cloth and show that the ball has disappeared. I'll cover my hand with the cloth again and ask everyone in the room to feel under the cloth and make sure the ball isn't there. Once again you'll be the last person to feel under the cloth. You'll secretly put the ball back in my hand. Then I'll lift the cloth and show that the ball has reappeared. You should act as if you're seeing the trick for the first time and you don't know the secret. Don't overdo it, though. Just do your thing in a relaxed and natural way. 99

Practice with your shill until you can both do your parts smoothly. No one will suspect a thing!

How to Do This Trick

66 An alien named Pluto (from Pluto, of course) visited me the other day. I told the alien that no one would believe this had happened to me. So it gave me a ball from Pluto and said in a strange accent

that if anyone doubts me, I should show the ball to prove that there's life on other planets. Are you a doubter? Good. That gives me a chance to show you Pluto's ball.

This is no ordinary ball. Sure, it looks ordinary, it smells ordinary, it even tastes ordinary (though I wouldn't try tasting it if I were you)–but it's not. It's from Pluto! Here, take a look. **99**

1. Hand the ball to the audience and encourage everyone to pass it around. Let everyone inspect your hands and the cloth, too. If you're wearing long sleeves, roll them up. Make it clear that you're not using any hidden gimmicks.

66 Now watch what this ball can do. **99**

2. Hold the ball in your palm-up hand and cover it with the cloth.

66 Each of you, please feel under the cloth and make sure the ball is there. **99**

3. The last person to feel under the cloth is your shill. He or she secretly takes the ball from your hand and either palms it or puts it in a pocket.

66 Alakapocus! **99**

4. Lift the cloth with a dramatic sweep of your hand. The ball has disappeared!

5. Let everyone inspect your hands and the cloth again.

6. Drape the cloth over your hand again.

66 Now please feel under the cloth and make sure the ball isn't there. **99**

7. The last person to feel under the cloth is your shill. He or she secretly puts the ball back in your palm.

66 Epplekedepple! **99**

8. You lift the cloth with a flourish again, and—voilà!—the ball has reappeared.

Banana Split

Illusion

You peel a banana. It's already sliced into seven pieces.

Props

Banana
Sewing needle
Marker

Getting Ready

An inch or so down from the top of the banana along one of its ridges, poke the needle into the banana and carefully wiggle it from side to side, slicing the banana in two. As you wiggle the needle, make sure you don't poke it through other

parts of the peel. Remove the needle, poke it into the banana a little farther down, and make another slice. Repeat this process four more times. You've now sliced the banana into seven pieces inside its peel. Write the number seven on the banana.

How to Do This Trick

1. Pick up the banana.

> **"** Food companies are always looking for new ways to get people to buy their stuff. Smucker's was doing fine selling jam; then they decided to mix in some peanut butter. Even fruit growers are getting into the act. How do they grow grapes without seeds? Now **that's** magic. I recently heard that some banana company has jumped on the bandwagon. You know how you have to slice a banana before you put it in your cereal? This company figured out a way to grow sliced bananas. I have no idea how they do it. See this number? **"**

2. Point to the number seven written on the banana.

> **"** It tells you how many pieces the banana is sliced into. Here, take a look. **"**

3. Peel the banana and show the seven pieces. Offer them to the audience or eat them yourself.

The Ring, the String, and Farfel

Illusion

A ring disappears from your hand, then—*kablooey!*—it reappears.

Props

Marker
Ring (borrowed from volunteer)
Two-foot length of string
Cup or pocket

How to Do This Trick

"Have you met my friend Farfel?"

1. Hold your left hand palm-down. Make a loose fist, tucking your thumb inside your fingers. You now have a hand puppet! Give your puppet a goofy name. (Let's say it's Farfel.) Your index finger is its upper lip, and your thumb is its lower lip. Wiggle your thumb up and down to make it look as if Farfel is speaking. Say Farfel's lines in a funny voice—something really high- or low-pitched. If you can do it without moving your lips, even better! (This skill is called ventriloquism.)

You: **"Farfel, how are you doing?"**
Farfel: **"I can't see! I can't see!"**
You: **"Ah, Farfel needs some eyes."**

2. Draw two eyes above Farfel's mouth.

You: **"Can you see now?"**
Farfel: **"A little."**
You: **"Good."**

3. Borrow a ring from a volunteer.

You: **"Farfel is going to swallow this ring."**
Farfel: **"I am?"**
You: **"Sure."**

4. Thread the string through the ring. Hold up the ends of the string with your right hand so the ring is dangling in the middle of the string.

You: **"Here you go, Farfel. Bon appétit!"**

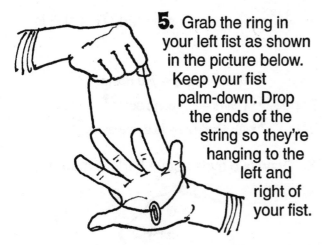

5. Grab the ring in your left fist as shown in the picture below. Keep your fist palm-down. Drop the ends of the string so they're hanging to the left and right of your fist.

Farfel: (garbled) **"Yuck. This tastes awful."**

You: **"Go ahead; swallow it."**

Farfel: **"I don't think so."**

6. With your right hand, grab the right end of the string and drape it over the back of your left fist so it hangs over the left side of your fist.

7. Now reach over your left fist and grab the other end of the string. As you do so, secretly drop the ring into your right hand.

Your right hand is now holding the ring and the string threaded through it. Drape the string across the back of your left fist so it crosses the string that's already there and hangs over the right side of your left fist. You're pulling the ring along the string at the same time—but the audience can't see the ring because it's hidden in your hand. Secretly pull the ring all the way off the string.

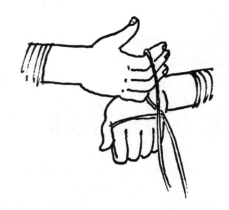

You: **"To keep Farfel from spitting out the ring before swallowing, please place your finger right on the spot where the ends of the string cross."**

8. Nod at the volunteer. The volunteer places a finger on the crossed strings.

Farfel: (still garbled) **" Hey, get your finger off my head! "**

You: **" Keep your finger there. Now, Farfel, swallow the ring. "**

Farfel: **Gulp.**

You: **" Did you swallow it? "**

Farfel: **" Yuck...yeah. "**

You: **" Let's find out. "**

9. Open your left hand and show that the ring has disappeared.

You: **" Well, look at that! "**

Farfel: **" I think I'm going to throw up. "**

You: **" Don't yak all over the floor! Here– "**

10. Give Farfel something to throw up in, like a cup or your pocket. As you pick up the cup or open your pocket with your right hand, secretly drop in the ring. Pretend Farfel is throwing up into the cup or pocket. Then fish out the ring and hand it to the volunteer.

You: **" I'm not sure if you want this anymore, since Farfel puked on it, but here it is anyway. Thank you. "**

This patter is just something my kooky imagination cooked up. If you think it's stupid, use your imagination to make up your own, or perform the trick without Farfel—it'll still be an amazing illusion.

(See pages 2–4 for more on character.)

Practice Tip

When you first grab the ring, hold it in the middle of your palm. Right before you drop it into your right hand, shift the ring to the left a bit. This will make the drop a lot easier. Practice the drop in front of a mirror until you can do it smoothly.

If you use Farfel, practice having conversations. Develop Farfel's character. (See pages 2–4 for more on character.) Before you know it, Farfel will be saying things even you don't expect!

George Washington Was Claustrophobic

Illusion

A quarter passes through a scarf.

Props

Two quarters
Scarf

How to Do This Trick

" George Washington was claustrophobic. That means he was afraid of small, enclosed spaces. This is not to be confused with santa-claustrophobia, which is a fear of Christmas. Since Georgie is on the U.S. quarter, some quarters are claustrophobic, too. Every now and then one starts hopping around in my pocket, trying to get out. If you put your ear up to a soda machine, you might hear a few Georgies clanking around in there, panicking, desperate for the open air. **"**

1. Show the quarters in the palm of your right hand.

" Here are two quarters. One is claustrophobic; the other isn't. See how they're enjoying the open air of my palm? But watch what happens when I drape this scarf over them. Now they're trapped. **"**

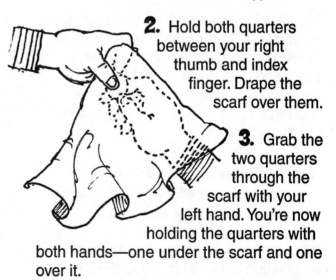

2. Hold both quarters between your right thumb and index finger. Drape the scarf over them.

3. Grab the two quarters through the scarf with your left hand. You're now holding the quarters with both hands—one under the scarf and one over it.

4. Pretend your right hand is letting go of the quarters, moving to the outside of the scarf, and grabbing the quarters through the scarf just like your left hand. As you do so, secretly remove one quarter from under the scarf, place it on the outside of the scarf next to the other quarter, and grab both quarters with both hands, adjusting the scarf so it hides the outside quarter from the audience's view. (Grab the cloth directly below the coin and fold it up over the coin.) Throughout this step, keep the scarf between the audience and your right hand so the audience can't see what your hand is doing. The audience thinks both quarters are still under the scarf.

5. Choose a volunteer from the audience.

> 66 Feel the quarters. They're pressed together in a tight space. One's happy; the other's not. One Georgie is already starting to panic. 99

6. Let the volunteer feel the quarters through the scarf. He or she thinks both are under the scarf.

> 66 I feel one trying to escape. Uh-oh. Here he comes—right through the scarf and into my hands! 99

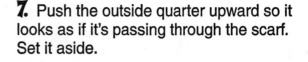

7. Push the outside quarter upward so it looks as if it's passing through the scarf. Set it aside.

> 66 The other one seems to be perfectly happy sitting all snug and cozy under the scarf. 99

8. Grab the inside quarter with your left hand and pull the scarf off it with the right hand to show that one quarter stayed under the scarf.

9. If you're a girl, take a bow. If you're a boy, do a nice curtsy.

Practice Tip

Practice this trick in front of a mirror, paying special attention to doing step 4 in a relaxed and natural way. Keep talking during this step to distract the audience.

When you make the coin appear, ham it up. Make it look as if the coin is struggling to get out from under the cloth. Push it up slowly to add drama.

CHAPTER 7
Gag Magic

Gag magic is a first cousin to "real" magic. They're both great ways to entertain people, but they're different in one important way.

When you do a real magic trick, you're trying to create an illusion—make your audience believe you're doing something amazing. When you do a gag magic trick, you just *pretend* that you're going to create an amazing illusion—and then you veer off and do something goofy.

Gag magic is like telling a joke. There's a punch line at the end of the trick, and when you get there, everyone either laughs or punches you in the nose. Gag magic takes no practice, and you don't have to work hard to fool people either. And you don't have to act goofy, because goofiness is built into gag magic.

Don't know what I'm talking about? You will after you read this chapter.

The Washcloth

Hold up a washcloth. Bet someone that if the two of you stand on opposite edges of the cloth, he or she won't be able to punch you in the nose.

If you're a scoundrel, you'll actually bet money. If you're a nice guy (or girl or ant), you'll just make a gentleman's (or gentle-woman's or gentleant's) bet.

Open a door and place the washcloth on the threshold. Have your pal stand on one edge of the washcloth. Close the door and stand on the opposite edge. Shout through the door, "Go ahead; punch me in the nose!"

Don't use a thin door, or you might actually get punched.

What's on the Paper?

Have a volunteer write something on a piece of paper, then fold it and put it on the table. Place a book (or rock or whatever) on the paper to prevent you from sneaking a look.

Bet the volunteer that you can say what's on the paper. Pretend to concentrate very hard.

"Aha!" you eventually say. "A book (or rock or whatever) is on the paper!"

Knock on Wood

Bet your brother that he'll get out from under a table before you knock on it three times. Your brother crawls under the table.

You knock once. "Are you getting out yet?" you ask.

"No," he says.

You knock again, then ask, "Are you getting out yet?"

"No way!" he says.

You say, "Before I knock a third time, you'll be out from under that table."

Your brother snickers because he thinks he's got you beat.

You say, "You know what? I don't think I'm going to knock on that table quite yet.

First I'm going to get something to eat." You walk off and stay away as long as it takes for your brother to get bored and come out. (I promise you he will sooner or later.) Then you walk over and knock on the table a third time.

My sister played this trick on me when I was six years old. The creep.

Both Sides Now

Tell your sister you can see both sides of a coin at once. Challenge her to try it first. If she holds the coin up to a mirror, tell her that doesn't count; she's seeing the reflection of one side, not the side itself.

When your sister gives up, take the coin back from her. Spin it on a table. As the spinning slows, you'll see both sides of the coin at once.

This is just an optical illusion, of course. You're really seeing one side at a time, but they're alternating so fast that it looks as if you're seeing them both at once.

Which Are Farthest?

Place three coins in a row on a table as shown in the picture below.

Ask someone to tell you which two coins are farthest apart. He or she will probably say that the middle coin and left coin or the middle coin and right coin are farthest apart.

Wrong! The answer is…drum roll, please…the two end coins are farthest apart!

Underwater Fire

Bet someone you can light a match underwater. Fill a glass with water, have your pal hold it, then light a match under it!

This doesn't give you license to start playing with matches. Don't be stupid and burn your home down, causing your parents to sue me and take all my earnings from this book as well as my life savings and reducing me to a bum begging on the street for dimes, while you…you…get rich from all my money and become a famous TV magician, and I have to watch you on TV through some department store window, thinking, "Ah, I could have been rich and famous like that—but I taught that kid to play with matches, and look where it's gotten me. Alas! Alas!"

So listen to me: Go ahead and do this gag if an adult gives you permission, but for goodness sake, be careful! I don't want to end up a bum.

Folding Challenge

Bet a friend that he or she can't fold a piece of paper nine times by halving the paper each time.

You can't fold *any* paper in this way more than eight times—try it!

Six Glasses

Here's great way to kill some time when you're at a restaurant waiting for your food or your bill or for your aunt Zelda to return from the bathroom.

Arrange six glasses in a row on the table. Fill the three glasses on the left with water. Ask the bored, "Can you make the glasses alternately full and empty by moving only one glass?"

Sometimes a smarty-pants will figure out the trick. (My friend Bob did.) But most folks will be stumped.

The trick is...another drum roll, please...lift up the second glass from the left and pour its water into the second glass from the right.

Three Glasses

Still waiting for Aunt Zelda? Yawn.

Arrange three glasses in a row on the table. Turn the middle glass upside down. (Make sure it's empty first, or you'll have a different kind of fun on your hands.) The left and right glasses should be right-side up.

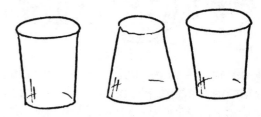

Say, "I can get all three glasses upside down on the table by making exactly three moves." Then do the following:

1. Turn over the middle and right glasses at the same time.

2. Turn over the left and right glasses at the same time.

3. Turn over the middle and right glasses at the same time.

All the glasses are now upside down.

Here's the sneaky part. Turn the middle glass right-side up and challenge Uncle Mortimer to do what you did—get all three glasses upside down in exactly three moves.

He'll probably try to copy your moves. But it won't work, because you arranged the cups differently for him than you did for yourself. He won't notice that, of course.

Napkin Quarters

Aunt Zelda's *still* in the bathroom? Is she ever going to come out so everyone can go home?

Put a quarter on the table and hand your cousin Schmendrick a paper napkin. Say, "I'll bet you can't tear this napkin into four equal pieces with only two tears. If you can. I'll give you a quarter."

Schmendrick, of course, easily tears the napkin into four equal pieces. So you hand him a quarter...a quarter of the napkin! Ha, ha.

Make sure you snatch your coin back quickly, or Schmendrick might beat you to it. You'd have a hard time getting it away from him—especially if he's your older cousin.

Heads, I Win; Tails, You Lose

Who leaves the tip? Why not flip a coin to decide? Before you flip, say, "Heads, I win; tails, you lose." Either way, you'll win.

Place the same coin heads-up under a glass. Cover the glass with a napkin. Bet your cousin Erwin that you can turn the coin tails-up without lifting the glass.

Have Erwin place his hand over the napkin to make him think he's preventing any funny business. Wait a few seconds, then say, "I win!"

When Erwin lifts the napkin and glass to see if you're right, immediately pick up the coin and flip it over. If he argues, tell him, "I did win! I didn't touch the glass; you did!"

Three French Fries

Ah, Aunt Zelda's back. Borrow a quarter from her and place it on the table. Arrange three French fries in a triangle around it. Bet Aunt Zelda a dime that she won't answer "three French fries" to all three questions you're going to ask her.

Ask Aunt Zelda, "If I have four French fries and take away one, how many are left?"

Aunt Zelda says, "Three French fries."

Ask Aunt Zelda, "What are surrounding the quarter on the table?"

Aunt Zelda says, "Three French fries."

Ask Aunt Zelda, "What will you take for your quarter?"

If she answers "three French fries," take the quarter and give her the fries. Give her a dime, too, because she wins the bet.

If she answers something else, she gets her quarter back, but she loses the bet and has to give you a dime.

No matter what she says, you come out richer. Now you can go to college.

Pain in the Neck

Bet someone that you can pour a glass of water down your neck without getting all wet.

How do you do it? Drink it!

Don't Judge a Book...

Bet your uncle Finklemeister that he can't hold a book at arm's length and shoulder height for ten minutes.

It's impossible to do—especially when you're ninety years old and arthritic like Uncle Finklemeister. It's impossible for Arnold Schwarzenegger, too!

4 – 1 = 5

Tell someone that four minus one equals five. When your pal protests, say that you can prove you're right.

Find an ordinary sheet of paper and a pair of scissors. Count the corners of the paper out loud in front of your pal. Then say, "I'll get rid of one corner, and you'll see: Four minus one equals five."

Cut off one corner of the paper. Now count the corners again. The paper now has five corners.

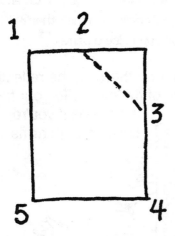

Tricky Picture

Challenge someone to draw the picture at left with one continuous line—without drawing over any line that's already drawn and without lifting the pencil from the paper.

When your victim gives up, show him or her how it's done:

What a Heel

Bet Grandpa Schmegeggi that he can't stand with both heels against the wall and pick up a coin on the floor in front of him. It's impossible—unless Gramps cheats!

The Flying Hat

This trick is a good one to do when you're hanging out at home with a friend. No fancy magic or sneaky bets here—this one's just plain old goofiness!

Illusion

Someone blows toward you, and your hat rises off your head and settles back down again.

Props

Hat
Wall mirror (at least two feet by two feet)

How to Do This Trick

1. Put the hat on your head.

2. Hold the mirror upright on a table. Sit at one edge of the mirror and press your nose against the edge.

3. Have your friend sit on the opposite side of the table from you in such a way that he or she can see only the reflective side of the mirror.

Ask your friend to hold the mirror in place. Let go of the mirror so both your hands are free.

4. Drum your fingers on the reflective side of the mirror and make a thoughtful face. To your friend it looks as if you're thinking hard while drumming the fingers of both hands against each other.

> **"**Hmm...you know what I'd have if I had seventy-two dollars in one pocket and ninety-six dollars in the other? Someone else's pants!**"**

5. Flap your arm that's on the reflective side of the mirror. To your friend it looks as if you're flapping both arms.

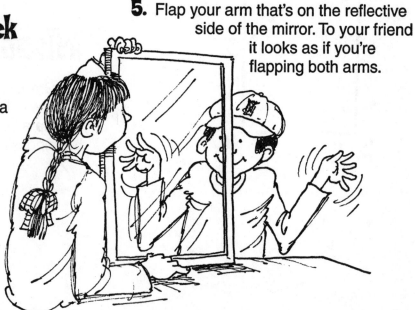

" I just flew in from L.A., and boy, are my arms tired! **"**

" Blow at me, please—nice and steady. **"**

6. As your friend blows at you, lift your hat a little with your hand that's behind the mirror. Shake the hat a bit to make it look as if it's being blown about.

" Blow harder. **"**

7. As your friend blows harder, lift your hat higher and shake it harder. When your friend stops blowing, settle the hat back on your head. To your friend it looks as if he or she has blown your hat right off your head and let it back down again.

Practice Tip

Practice this trick with two mirrors. Have someone hold the first mirror as described in step 3 and hold the second mirror in front of him or her, so the reflective side is facing you. The second mirror will let you see what your friend should be seeing in this trick.

After you perfect the moves I've suggested, try to come up with some of your own.

CHAPTER 8
How to Learn More Tricks

Other Magicians

Here's how you can find out how to do a trick you've seen someone else perform—maybe onstage or in a bar. (Hey, what's a kid like you doing in a bar? Get out of there.)

Approach the magician after the act is over and everyone else in the audience has gone or is no longer paying attention. Magicians never reveal their tricks to people who are just curious, so make it clear that you're a serious, working magician and not just some smart aleck.

Because you're a kid, the magician might not believe you. If that happens, prove you're a real magician by talking shop. Yammer on about key cards, false shuffles, palming, and other stuff that only a magician would know. This should convince the magician that you're the real McCoy.

Once you've done that, you're in. Magicians love to talk to other magicians. When real estate agents get together, they talk real estate. Musicians talk music. Magicians talk magic. If you've presented yourself as a mature young performer, the magician will probably be more than happy to talk to you for a while.

Never come right out and ask a magician how to do a trick. Talk around it instead. Let's say the magician just performed a rope trick. Ask what the trick is called. Then ask where he or she got it. Did it come from a particular book or magic shop? If you know a similar trick, share it with the magician. Then, if you're really lucky, he or she might tell you the secret. It all depends on how secretive the magician is.

If you want to learn a trick that you've seen on TV, of course you can't approach the magician after the show. Go to your

local magic store and describe the trick to a salesperson. The trick (instructions, props, and all) may be for sale at the store. Or the salesperson may direct you to a book that explains the trick. If there are no magic stores near you, call one on the phone instead. (Ask an adult for permission first.) Almost all magic stores sell stuff by mail order.

Magic Stores

A magic store is a valuable tool for any magician. To get the most out of your local magic store, you might want to follow my lead....

I try to develop a relationship with one of the salespeople at a store. I begin by saying that I have money to spend. Hanging out in magic stores can be fun and is usually allowed, but if the salespeople know you intend to spend money there, they'll treat you much more respectfully.

Then I describe the trick I'm looking for and my other needs. For instance, I say, "I'm looking for a mind-reading trick. It needs to cost less than twenty dollars, it needs to be funny, and it has to pack small and play big. I have too many card tricks already, so don't show me any of those. And I don't want a trick that's so hard, I'll have to practice it for weeks before I perform it." If I'm looking for a trick I saw on TV, I ask if the store sells it and how much it costs.

If the salesperson's any good, he or she starts demonstrating tricks for me. (It's like getting a free magic show!) I buy the ones I like. Then the salesperson tells me the secrets.

Sometimes at magic stores you pay twenty bucks or more for stuff like a piece of rope with a magnet hidden in it. You might feel ripped off. But remember: You're paying not just for the prop, but also for the secret. And secrets can be worth a lot.

Magic Clubs

Another great way to learn new tricks is to join a magic club. There's usually a magic club in or around any big town. For a small yearly fee, you can join a local club and schmooze with other magicians who live near you. Often clubs bring in famous magicians for lectures. They may also hold prop auctions and member demonstrations. Usually the members of a magic club share their secrets.

But be warned: Some magic clubs won't allow kids to join. If your local club is one of these, you can still belong to a magic club. The two biggest clubs in the United States, the Society of American Magicians (SAM) and the International Brotherhood of Magicians (IBM), both offer special memberships just for kids. Hop online (with an adult's permission) and visit SAM at http://www.magicsam.com or IBM at http://www.magician.org. You may find a branch of one of these clubs in your nearest city. If not, you could subscribe to one of their magazines, where you'll find lots of helpful hints.

Of course, you could always start your own club. That's what I did when I was a kid. My father and I started a magic club together one rainy afternoon when I was only six. It was fun!

Magic Web Sites

Surfing the Internet is another excellent way to see what's out there. Check with an adult first, then go to any search engine and type in the word *magic.* Then jump in and wade through the web sites that come up. Many magic stores have web sites, and some of them will answer questions you e-mail to them.

Magic Books

And finally, you can learn magic through books—like this one! Any library will have lots of books on magic (unless they've disappeared!).

Remember: Just because something is in a book doesn't mean it's good. Some magic books are fun, easy to understand, and contain really dynamite tricks. Others are bummers. Use your noodle and find the books that are right for you.

At the end of *Hocus Jokus* you'll find a bibliography. That's a list of books I used to help me write this one. Most of the books I used are out of print. (That means no more new ones are being made.) But you should still be able to find them in libraries and on the Internet.

CHAPTER 9
Good-bye

I had fun writing this book. I hope you had fun reading it! If I did my job well, you now know a bit about character, style, showmanship, patter, props, and humor—*and* you've learned a whole bunch of funny tricks. I want to stress (there's that word again!) that this book is just a starting point for you.

Sure, you can use my ideas exactly the way I've explained them, but I hope you come up with your own funny ideas, too. That way when you perform, people won't be mumbling, "That magician's pretty good, but he (or she) reminds me of someone. Oh, I know: that Charney guy."

You can do it; I know you can. Don't be afraid to ham it up. Try new ideas even if they seem crazy. You can't overdo it, remember?

Work hard. Write good ideas down so you don't forget them. Constantly look for ways to perfect your craft.

When people clap or compliment you, just say "thank you very much" and smile. You don't need to do anything else.

Be kind to your audience; you need them. Act as if you genuinely like and respect them—which is a lot easier to do if you really do like and respect them.

Relax and look like you're having fun. Smile a lot and mean it. Smiles are contagious. My show improved greatly when I started smiling along with my audiences. They liked me more, became more relaxed, and were more willing to forgive bad jokes and mistakes. And I enjoyed myself more, too!

Eat your vegetables. Don't watch too much TV. Do well in school. Stop picking your nose. Clean up your room. Listen, you young whipper-snapper, do you want to get grounded? Then stop hitting your brother....

CHAPTER 10
What's So Funny?

This is a bonus chapter. I've tacked it onto the end of this book because not only is it pretty boring, it's not that important. It's also kind of grown-up. So feel free to just ignore it. If you do decide to keep reading, maybe you'll learn something…or not. Doesn't matter.

We all know what's funny. Most of us don't need to figure out *why* certain things are funny. But I'm obsessed with humor, man. I have to pick it apart. I can't help it.

So what makes something funny? (Hey, that reminds me of a joke: Why didn't the cannibal eat the clown? Because the clown tasted funny. Ooh boy.) I'd like to spend a page or two (or three or four or five or six or—stop that, Charney) dissecting (taking apart and studying) this funny thing called humor. (Don't worry; it'll be a lot cleaner than dissecting frogs. Have you done that yet in school? Do seventh graders still have to dissect frogs? I'm gonna puke just thinking about it….)

There are whole books on this topic. Here's what I've come up with from all the stuff I've read and from my own experience. Take it or leave it.

How Humor Happens

The human brain loves patterns. As we go about our lives, we begin to realize that when we start at A, we usually end up at B. Eventually whenever we start at A, we expect to end up at B. Humor happens when we unexpectedly land at C instead.

Let's say someone tells you, "You have beautiful hair…." That's point A. Your brain takes you straight to point B: You assume that the person is paying you a compliment because he or she thinks highly of you. But then the person says, "…coming from each nostril!" Surprise!

It's the surprise that makes you laugh. Suddenly you see things differently from how you saw them a few seconds ago. If you'd already been talking about noses or if you'd heard this joke before, it wouldn't make you laugh.

The surprise creates a new idea in your mind. Of course you already know that hair grows in other places besides on people's heads. You just hadn't thought of it until it was pointed out to you.

The new idea is silly—but not so silly that you don't "get" it. The idea of hair coming from your nostrils is silly because you probably don't really have hairy nostrils, but it's not complete nonsense because it's at least possible for a person to have hairy nostrils. If the jokester had said "you have beautiful hair…coming from the toaster," you wouldn't have laughed because the comment would have been too nonsensical.

Finally, you can laugh at the nose hair joke because it doesn't threaten you. After all, you don't really have a nose hair problem. But let's say you do have an ear hair problem. If the joke had been about ear hair, you'd have known the jokester was being mean (or just stupid and thoughtless), and you'd have been too nervous or angry to laugh.

Sometimes it's hard to know what will threaten someone. Plus, what threatens one person may be perfectly fine for someone else. But be aware that dirty jokes and jokes about different cultures often offend people. It's best to just avoid that kind of humor.

Glossary

bon appétit: (French) Enjoy your meal.

Burton, Lance: (1960–) Famous magician who is known for performing traditional magic tricks and for his graceful, gentlemanly style.

Capisce?: (Italian) Understand?

character: The unique person a magician pretends to be while performing.

Chinese rings: Solid metal rings that appear to link and unlink effortlessly and magically. Any number or size of rings may be used. Tricks using Chinese rings have been traced back three thousand years.

Copperfield, David: (1956–) Born David Kotkin. Famous magician who has performed tricks like making the Statue of Liberty vanish and floating across the Grand Canyon. David Copperfield is known for his soft-spoken, charming, and witty style.

cups and balls: Props used in what's considered the oldest known type of magic trick. The balls seem to appear, disappear, and pass through the cups.

cut: To divide a deck of cards in half and place the bottom half on top of the other half.

false shuffle: Technique in which a magician pretends to mix up a deck of cards so the cards are arranged in a random order. In truth, the magician controls one or more cards while shuffling.

flourish: Dramatic motion.

force: (Usually refers to card tricks.) To make a volunteer choose a certain card. The volunteer, however, thinks he or she has free choice.

French drop: Technique in which a magician holds a coin between the thumb and index finger of the right hand, then pretends to grab the coin with the left hand while secretly dropping the coin into the right palm.

gimmick: Gadget used to trick people.

gullible: Easy to fool. (Did you know that the word *gullible* isn't in the dictionary? If you believe that, you're gullible.)

heckler: Person who pesters a magician while he or she is performing.

Houdini, Harry: (1874–1926) Born Erik Weisz. Famous magician known for his daring escapes and for exposing con artists who'd been fooling the public for years.

illusion: False image.

Japanese rings: My attempt at a joke. Japanese rings, as far as I know, don't exist. Except on the pay phones in Tokyo.

key card: Card memorized by a magician and handled so that it ends up on top of a card chosen by a volunteer. A key card tells the magician which card is the chosen card.

magician's choice: Magic trick in which a magician forces a volunteer to choose a certain item. The volunteer, however, thinks he or she has free choice.

mime: Actor who tells a story without words by using body movements and facial expressions.

misdirection: Distracting people from objects or actions one doesn't want them to notice.

novelty store: Store that sells unusual toys and trinkets.

palming: Hiding an object in the palm of one's hand.

pass: To secretly switch the bottom and top halves of a deck of cards.

patter: Anything a magician says during a magic trick that makes it more interesting for the audience.

Penn and Teller: Penn Jillette (1955–) and Raymond Teller (1948–), a famous team of funny magicians. Penn and Teller are known for poking fun at traditional magic.

poster putty: Rubbery material used to stick things together. Poster putty can be removed easily without ruining whatever it's stuck to.

prop: Any object that helps a magician perform a magic trick.

punch line: Funny and surprising ending of a joke.

pupik: (Yiddish) Bellybutton.

Rastafarian: Member of a religious group that started in Jamaica. Many Rastafarians wear a hairstyle called dreadlocks.

ribbon-spread: To set a deck of cards on a table and slide the top of the deck to the right to make a row of overlapping cards.

riffle: To raise one edge of a deck of cards and release the cards very quickly one by one.

schmo: Stupid or unpleasant person.

schnook: Stupid or gullible person.

shaved deck: Deck of cards with one side trimmed slightly at an angle. When a magician removes a card, reverses it, and places it back in the deck, it doesn't line up with the rest of the cards and is easy to locate.

shill: Magician's helper who's in on the trick.

showmanship: Anything a magician does to keep an audience's attention and interest.

shuffle: To mix up a deck of cards so the cards are arranged in a random order.

silks: Pieces of cloth made of silk.

sleight of hand: Move performed in a magic trick so quickly, skillfully, or sneakily that the audience can't see how it's done.

Spanish drops: Another corny joke. Also a light rain in Madrid.

stage presence: The ability to look and feel comfortable onstage.

style: How a magician's character behaves.

swami: Hindu religious teacher.

thumbtip: Flesh-colored plastic shell worn on the tip of a magician's thumb and used to hide small objects.

trance: Condition in which someone is only half-conscious and unaware of his or her surroundings.

ventriloquism: The art of throwing one's voice so it seems to be coming from elsewhere, such as a puppet. Many magicians are ventriloquists.

Bibliography

Allen, Harry. *Sleight of Foot in Mouth.* Daytona Beach, Fla.: n.p., 1985.

Allen, Harry. *Sleight of Lips.* Daytona Beach, Fla.: n.p., 1986.

Allen, Harry. *Sleight of Tongue.* Daytona Beach, Fla.: n.p., 1982.

Allen, Harry. *Sleight of Tongue in Cheek.* Daytona Beach, Fla.: n.p., 1984.

Dunninger, Joseph. *Dunninger's Complete Encyclopedia of Magic.* Secaucus, N.J.: Lyle Stuart, 1967.

Even More Remarkable Names. Edited by John Train. New York: Clarkson N. Potter, 1979.

The Friars Club Encyclopedia of Jokes. Edited by H. Aaron Cohl. New York: Black Dog and Leventhal Publishers, 1997.

Ginn, David. *Laughter Legacy.* Lilburn, Ga.: Scarlett Green Publications, 1998.

Glover, Russ. *Dr. Chang Presents Kneeslappers and Gaggers.* Silver Spring, Md.: Russel J. Glover, 1993.

Hay, Henry. *The Amateur Magician's Handbook.* New York: Signet, 1950.

Hugard, Jean, and Frederick Braué. *The Royal Road to Card Magic.* Cleveland and New York: World Publishing Company, 1951.

Kaye, Marvin. *The Stein and Day Handbook of Magic.* New York: Stein and Day, 1973.

Linkletter, Art. *Kids Say the Darndest Things.* Englewood Cliffs, N.J.: Prentice-Hall, 1957.

Lorayne, Harry. *The Magic Book.* New York: Putnam, 1977.

Mulholland, John. *Mulholland's Book of Magic.* New York: Charles Scribner's Sons, 1963.

Okal, Bill. *Card Magic.* New York: Paragon-Reiss, 1982.

Remarkable Names of Real People. Edited by John Train. New York: Clarkson N. Potter, 1977.

Rigney, Francis J. *A Beginner's Book of Magic.* Old Greenwich, Conn.: Devin-Adair, 1964.

Schindler, George. *Magic with Everyday Objects.* New York: Stein and Day, 1976.

Thurston, Howard. *400 Tricks You Can Do.* Garden City, N.Y.: Garden City Books, 1948.

World's Best Clown Gags. Edited by Clettus Musson. Flosso-Hornmann Magic, n.d.

Youngman, Henny. *Henny Youngman's Bar Bets, Bar Jokes, Bar Tricks.* New York: Carol Publishing Group, 1974.

Index

Also from Meadowbrook Press

✦ **The Aliens Have Landed!**
Author Kenn Nesbitt, a brilliant new star in the poetry galaxy, writes with the rhythmic genius of Jack Prelutsky and the humor of Bruce Lansky. Children will love the imaginative world of Kenn Nesbitt, a world with mashed potatoes on the ceiling, skunks falling in love, antigravity machines, and aliens invading the school—all wonderfully brought to life in illustrations by Margeaux Lucas.

✦ **Kids Pick the Funniest Poems**
Three hundred elementary-school kids will tell you that this book contains the funniest poems for kids—because they picked them! Not surprisingly, they chose many of the funniest poems ever written by favorites like Shel Silverstein, Jack Prelutsky, Jeff Moss, and Judith Viorst (plus poems by lesser-known writers that are just as funny). This book is guaranteed to please children ages 6–12!

✦ **Long Shot**
Eleven-year-old Laurie Bird Preston leaves her town, friends, and basketball teammates when her father takes a job in another city. Laurie faces a new school, new teammates, and new challenges, but she discovers that with time, understanding, and help from a quirky kid named Howard, fitting in may not be such a long shot.

✦ **No More Homework! No More Tests!**
The funniest collection of poems about school by the most popular children's poets, including Shel Silverstein, Jack Prelutsky, Bruce Lansky, David L. Harrison, Colin McNaughton, Kalli Dakos, and others who know how to find humor in any subject.

✦ **If Pigs Could Fly...**
A second collection of rip-roaring, side-splitting, rolling-in-the-aisles poems from Bruce Lansky that'll make kids grin, giggle, and howl.

✦ **What Do You Know About Manners?**
A book about manners that kids will enjoy reading? Absolutely, and parents will love it, too. Filled with fun, imaginative ways to fine-tune a child's manners, presented in a humorous format with over 100 quiz items and illustrations.

We offer many more titles written to delight, inform, and entertain.
To order books with a credit card or browse our full
selection of titles, visit our web site at:

www.meadowbrookpress.com

or call toll-free to place an order, request a free catalog, or ask a question:

1-800-338-2232

Meadowbrook Press • 5451 Smetana Drive • Minnetonka, MN • 55343